How to Draw for Minecrafters

A Step by Step Guide

MARK MULLE

Author's Note

This book is for your own pleasure. The characters in this coloring book such as Steve, Enderman or Herobrine... etc are based on the Minecraft Game coming from Minecraft ®/TM & © 2009-2024 Mojang / Notch.

This book is not authorized, endorsed by or affiliated with Mojang / Notch or its subsidiaries.

No part of this publication may be copied, reproduced in any format, by any means, electronic or otherwise, without prior consent from the copyright owner and publisher of this book.

Do you want to learn how to draw Minecraft stuff?

This guide will show you how to draw 50 different mobs, tools and other stuff from Minecraft starting from scratch to its final details. Some of the characters and items are easy to draw and some are a little challenging, but as you will discover in the book everything starts from squares and lines. So as long as you can draw squares, circles and lines you'll be able to draw these awesome stuff.

So what are you waiting for?
1. Sharpen your pencil
2. Get your paper
3. Have an eraser too to erase errors and to remove line guides
4. Grab your crayons so you can also color your masterpiece
5. and last of all Have fun!!!

MAGMA CUBE

1 THIS IS SUPER EASY, SO LET'S BEGIN.
FIRST, DRAW A FUNNY SHAPED SQUARE.

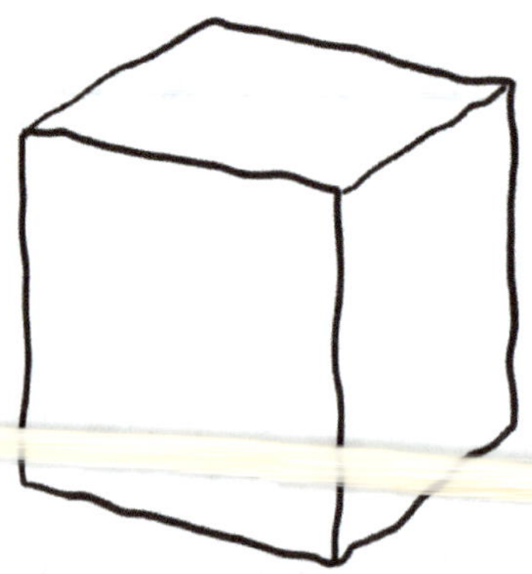

2 NOW FORM A CUBE BY ADDING THE SIDES
OF THE SQUARE.

3 ALMOST DONE! DRAW IT A FACE AND SOME
DETAILS TO MAKE YOUR MAGMA CUBE SUPER HOT!

BED

1 LET'S START WITH THIS SHAPE. IT IS A LARGE RECTANGULAR PRISM.

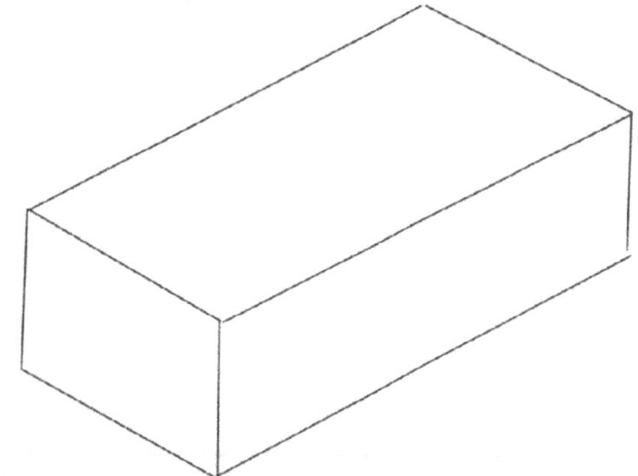

2 SHAPE YOR BED AND ITS LEGS BY FOLLOWING NEXT SIMPLE STEP. ERASE DOTTED LINE.

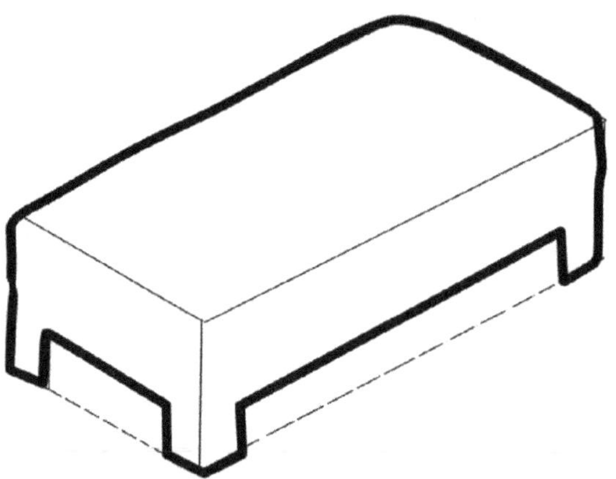

3 ALMOST DONE! NOW YOU CAN DRAW THE BLANKET AND SEPARATE THE PARTS OF THE BED.

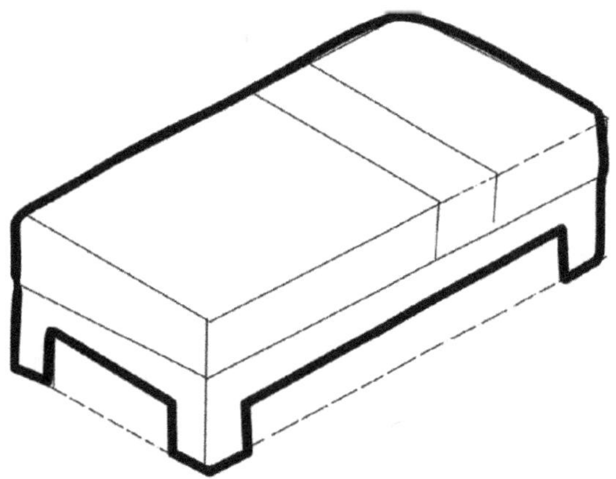

4 ALMOST DONE! USE THINNER LINES TO DRAW PILLOW AND SMALL DETAILS, AND YOU HAVE A COZY BED!

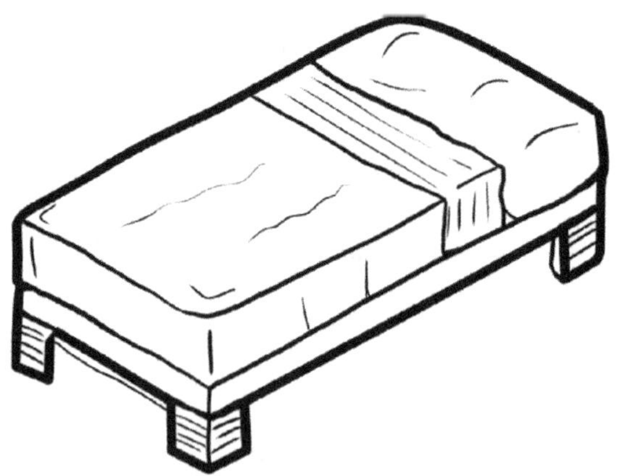

ENDER-CHEST

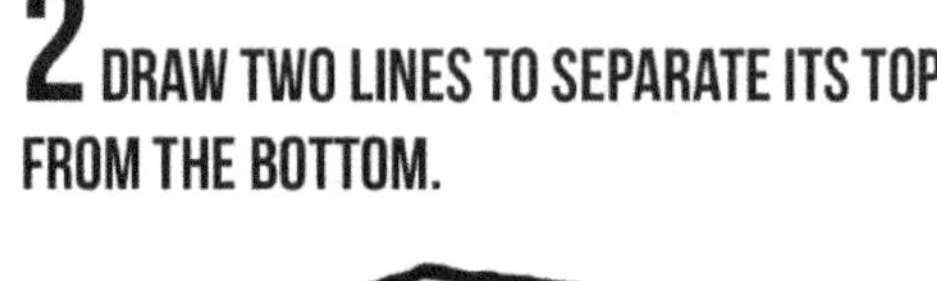

1 TO FORM THE SHAPE OF AN ENDER-CHEST, LET'S START WITH ONE BIG, BORING CUBE!

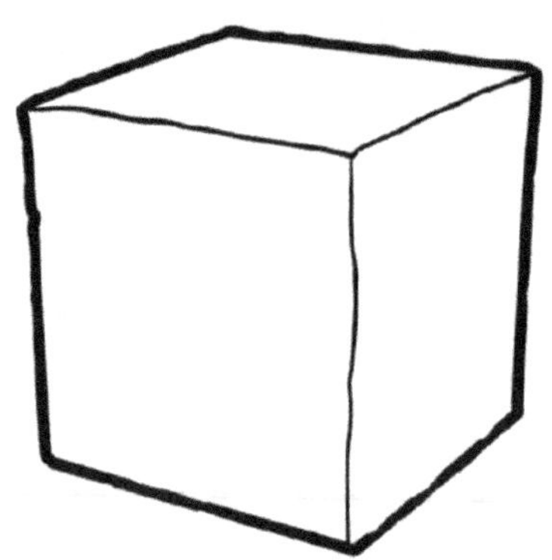

2 DRAW TWO LINES TO SEPARATE ITS TOP FROM THE BOTTOM.

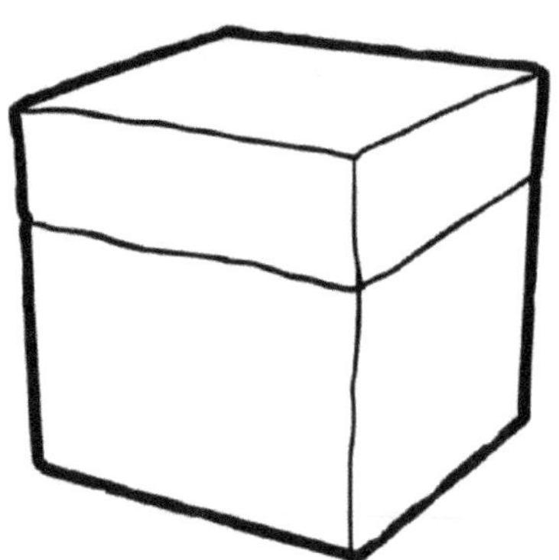

3 NOW, LET'S DRAW IT A LOCK. IT LOOKS LIKE A SMALL RECTANGULAR CUBOID, LYING AT THE MIDDLE LINE WHICH SEPARATES THE TOP FROM THE BOTTOM.

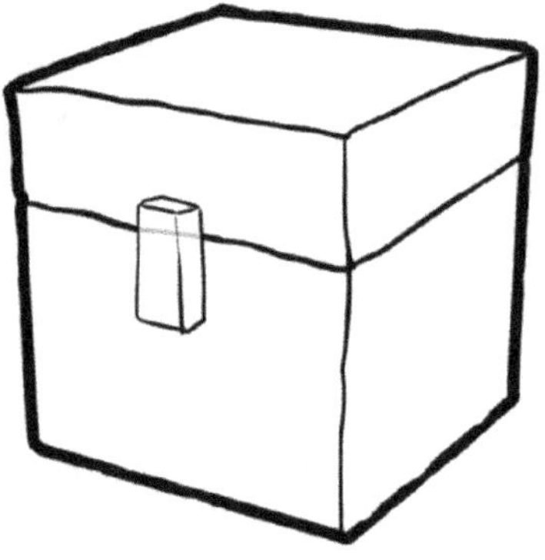

4 ALMOST DONE! NOW YOU CAN FINISH YOUR IMAGE BY ADDING DETAILS ON YOUR ENDER-CHEST.

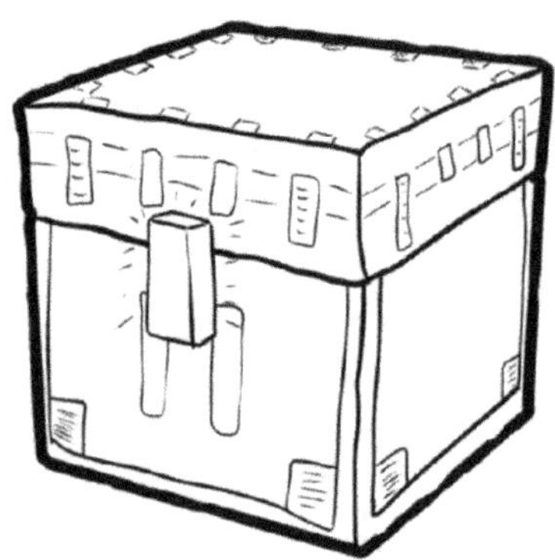

CREEPER

1 HEY, THIS ONE IS REALLY EASY TOO. THE CREEPER IS BASICALLY MADE FROM CUBES AND RECTANGULAR CUBOIDS. SO, LET'S START WITH DRAWING A CUBE FOR ITS HEAD AND A RECTANGULAR CUBOID FOR ITS BODY.

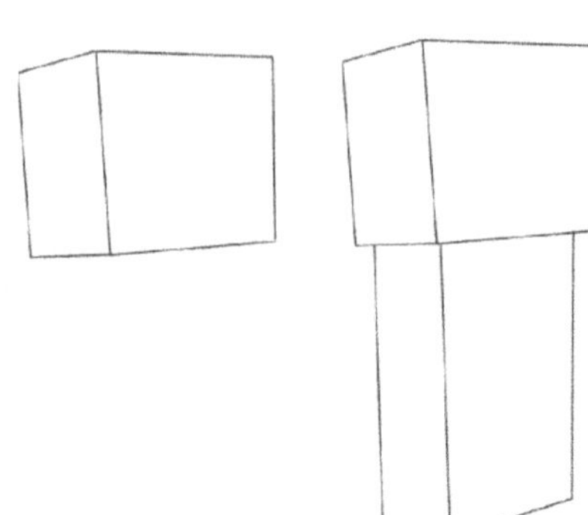

2 TO DRAW ITS LEGS, FOLLOW THESE STEPS: FIRST, DRAW A CUBE FOR ITS FIRST LEG. AFTER THAT DRAW TWO MORE CUBES. AT THIS POINT, YOU HAVE THE SHAPE OF ITS BODY.

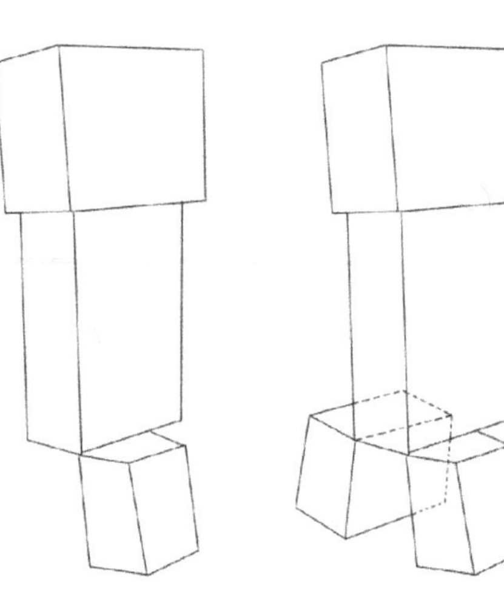

3 ALMOST DONE! NOW YOU CAN FINISH YOUR DRAWING BY OUTLINING THE EDGES WITH THICKER LINES, ADDING ITS FACE, MOUTH AND SOME OTHER DETAILS WHICH WILL MAKE THE CREEPER LOOK SCARY.

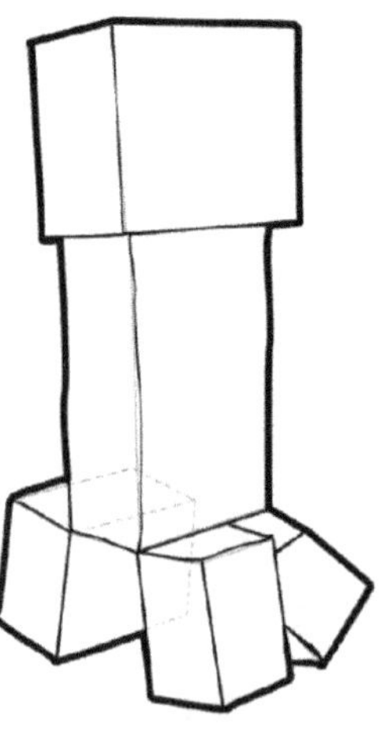

1 LET'S DRAW A BOOK. START BY DRAWING A PARALLELOGRAM AS LINE GUIDE. IN STEP 1A, TRACE THE OUTLINE OF THE BOOK

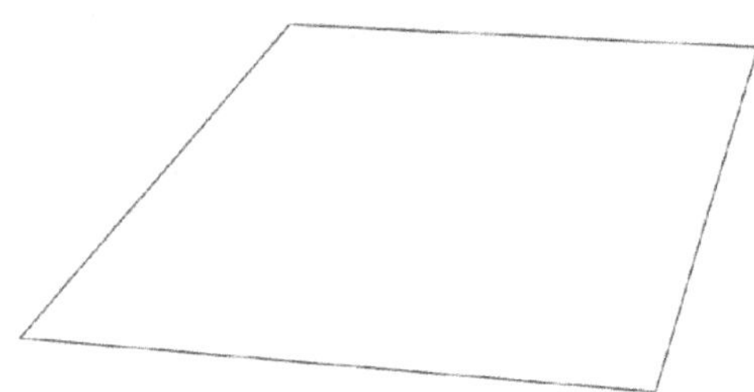

2 DRAW A THIN CUBOID AT THE BOTTOM AND AT THE EDGE OF THE BOOK AS LINE GUIDES. IN STEP 2A, DRAW A MIDDLE VERTICAL LINE ON THE BOOK TO MAKE ITS PAGES AND ADD CURVE LINES AT THE BOTTOM.

3 REMOVE THE LINE GUIDES OF THE BOOK. TO MAKE YOUR DRAWING LOOK MORE REALISTIC, WRITE AND DRAW ANYTHING ON THE PAGES OF THE BOOK.

JUKEBOX

1 START WITH A CUBE, JUST LIKE THIS ONE:

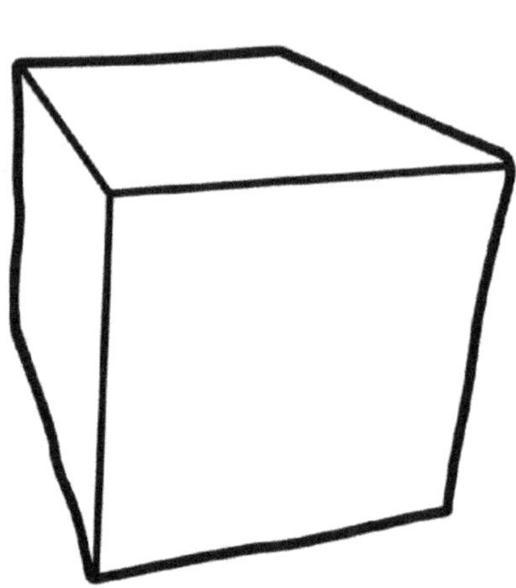

2 DRAW THICKER LINES ON ITS EDGES AND HORIZONTAL LINES ON TOP OF THE CUBE.

3 ALMOST DONE! FINISH OFF THIS DRAWING BY ADDING DETAILS ON THE BODY OF THE JUKEBOX

ANVIL

DIFFICULTY LEVEL

1 OKAY, THESE STEPS ARE EASY SO LET'S BEGIN. FIRST, DRAW A THIN RECTANGLE. DRAW ANOTHER RECTANGLE BELOW THE FIRST ONE BUT THIS RECTANGLE IS THICKER AS SHOWN IN IMAGE 1A. FEEL FREE TO REMOVE THE DOTTED LINES.

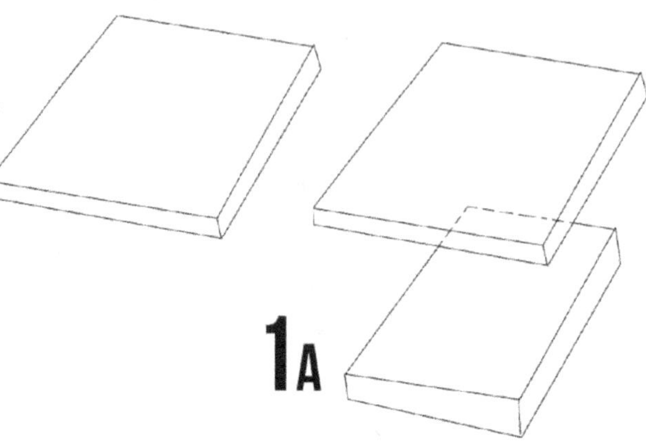

1A

2 DRAW TWO LINES CONNECTING YOUR TWO RECTANGLES TO FORM THE FINAL SHAPE OF YOUR ANVIL. ADD THE HORN OF THE ANVIL AS SHOWN IN 2A.

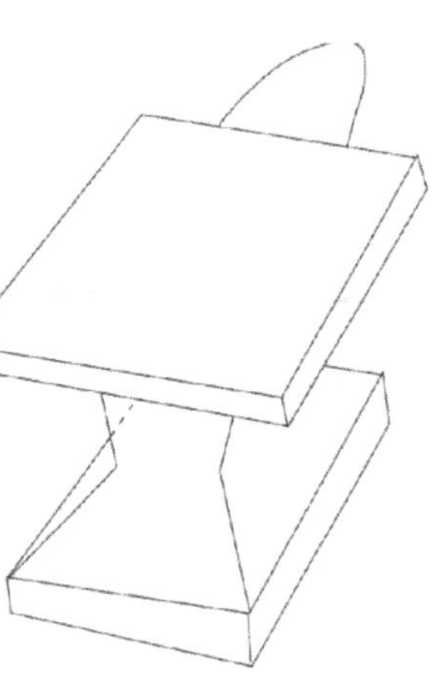

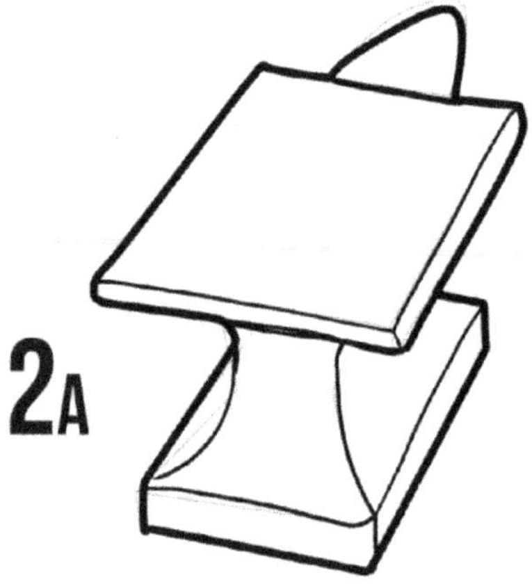

2A

3 ALMOST DONE! ADD SOME DETAILS ON YOUR ANVIL TO MAKE IT LOOK REALISTIC.

ENCHANTMENT TABLE

1 LET'S START OFF BY DRAWING A BOX. THEN ADD TWO CUBOIDS ON TOP OF THE BOX NEAR THE UPPER EDGE AS SHOWN IN IMAGE 1A.

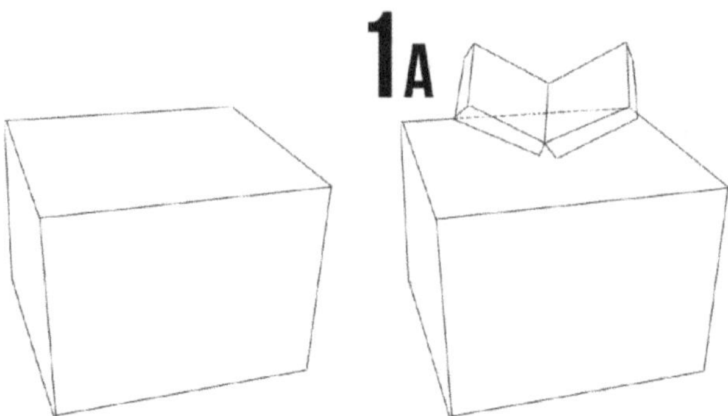

2 AT THIS STAGE, LET'S DRAW SOMETHING THAT LOOKS ROUGHLY LIKE AN OPEN BOOK. THEN DRAW THE BOOK COVER AND DRAW ONE PAGE OF THE BOOK AS SHOWN IN IMAGE 2A. SHADE THE OUTER LINES OF THE BOOK AND THE ENCHANTMENT TABLE.

3 ADD DETAILS ON YOUR ENCHANTMENT TABLE AND PUT WRITINGS OR DRAWINGS ON YOUR BOOK TO FINISH OFF THE IMAGE.

1 OK, THIS IS EASY. SO LETS BEGIN. DRAW THIS SHAPE.

2 NOW TO MAKE IT LOOK LIKE A CAKE, DRAW ITS SIDES AND ADD CREAM ON TOP.

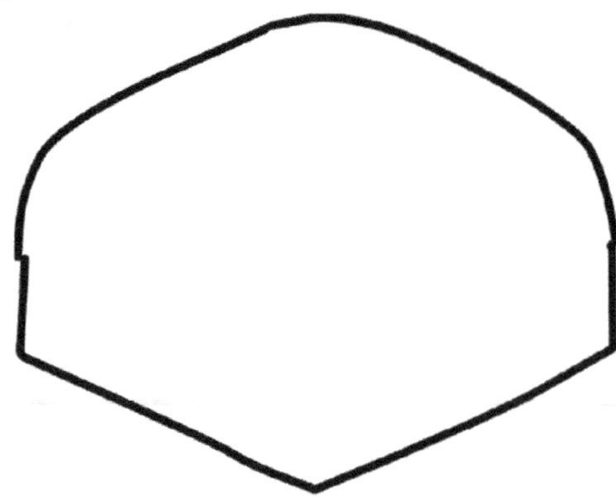

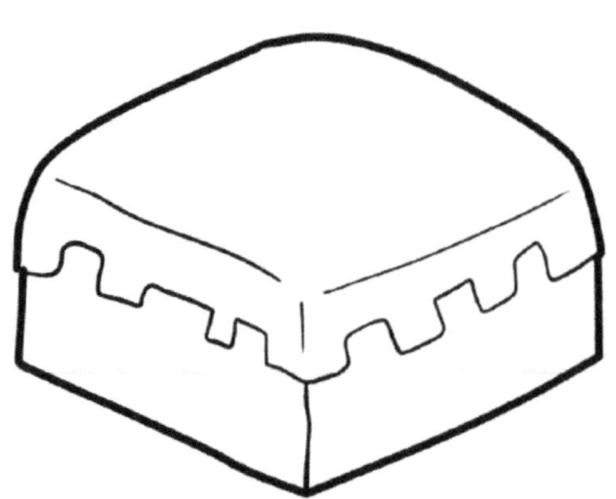

3 ALMOST DONE! ALL YOU HAVE TO DO IS DRAW A CANDLE AND ADD DETAILS AND SHADINGS ON YOUR CAKE.

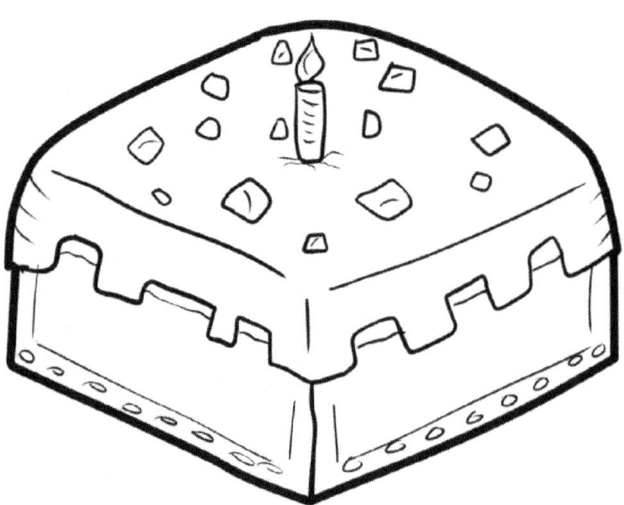

ALEX

DIFFICULTY LEVEL

1 LET'S START OFF BY DRAWING ALEX'S HEAD. DRAW A CUBE, THEN ADD THICKER LINES TO THE CUBE AND FINALLY ADD ALEX'S HAIR BANGS AND EAR.

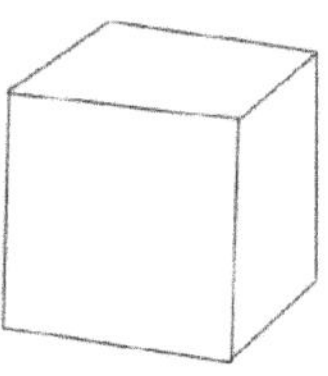  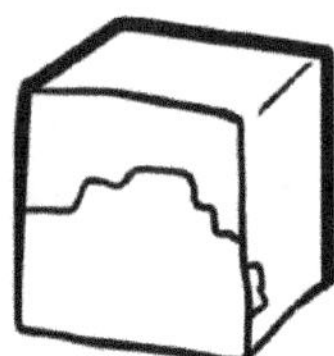

2 TO MAKE ALEX'S TORSO, DRAW A CUBOID BELOW ALEX'S HEAD. DRAW ALEX'S ARMS AT THE SIDES OF HER TORSO AS YOU CAN SEE IN STEP 2A.

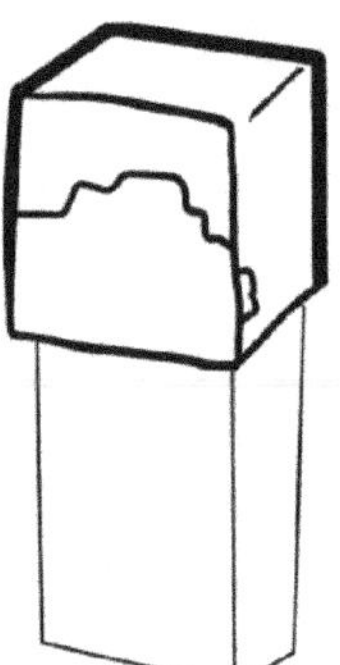

2 A

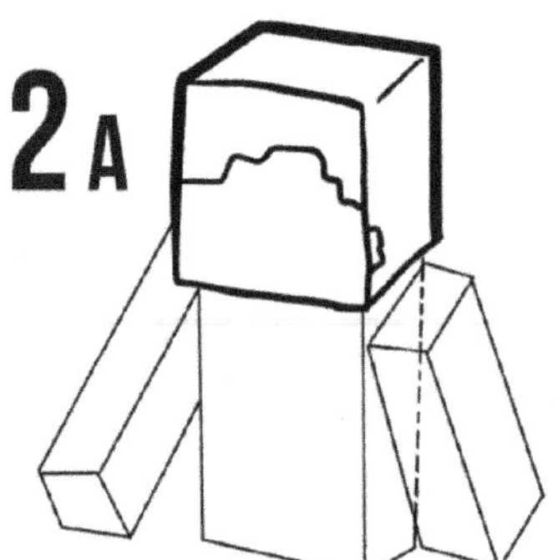

3 AT THIS STAGE, DRAW TWO RECTANGULAR CUBOIDS BELOW ALEX'S TORSO FOR HER LEGS.

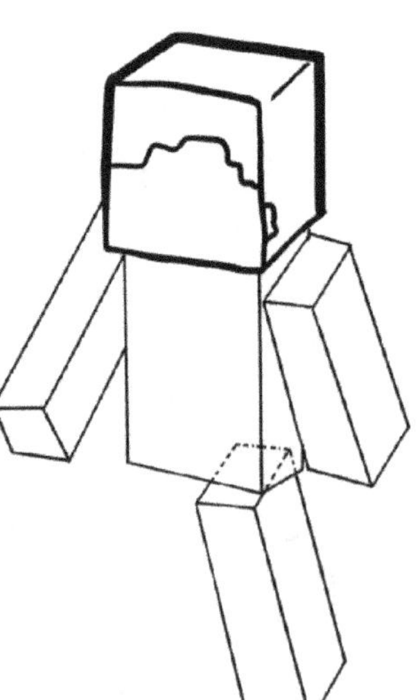 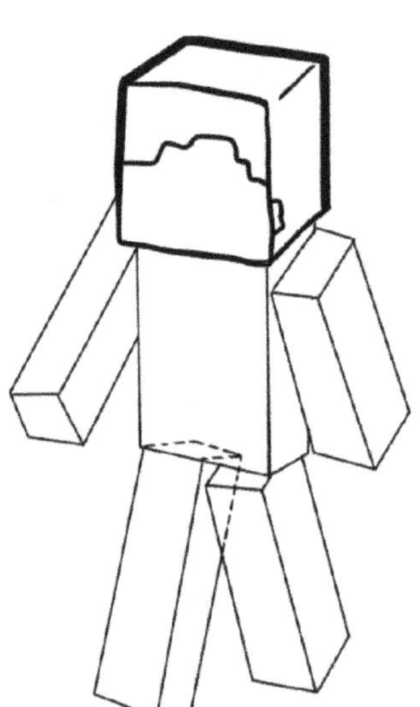

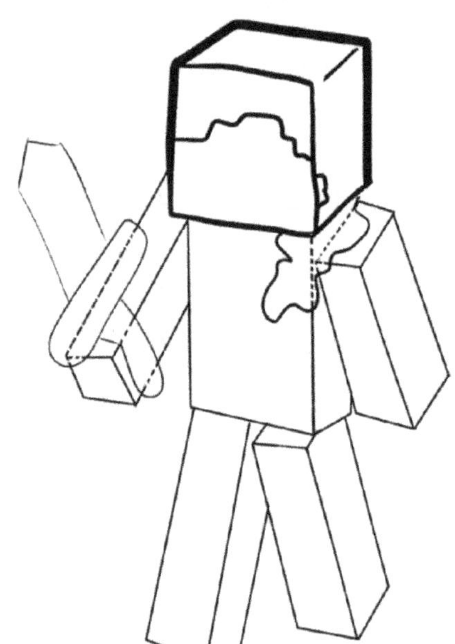

4 NOW THAT HER BODY IS COMPLETE, LET'S DRAW A SWORD ON HER RIGHT HAND.

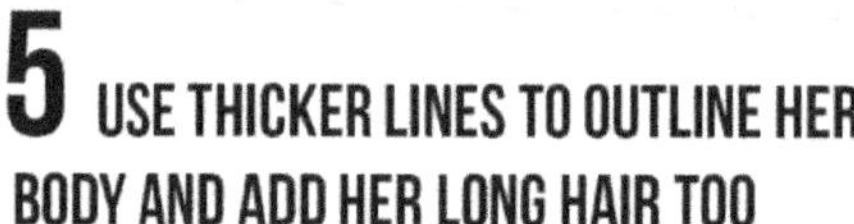

5 USE THICKER LINES TO OUTLINE HER BODY AND ADD HER LONG HAIR TOO

6 TO FINISH DRAWING ALEX, ADD HER EYES, NOSE AND MOUTH. ADD SOME SHADING AND OTHER DETAILS ON HER CLOTHES AND HAIR.

DRAGON

1 LET'S START OF BY DRAWING THE DRAGON'S HEAD. BEGIN WITH A BOX SHAPE FOR ITS HEAD AND DRAW ANOTHER BOX FOR ITS SNOUT. THEN DRAW ITS EARS AND NOSTRILS.

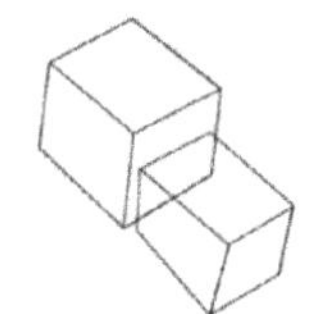 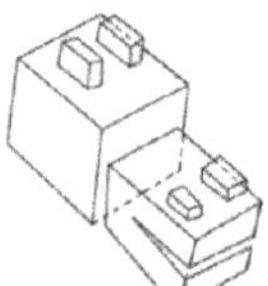 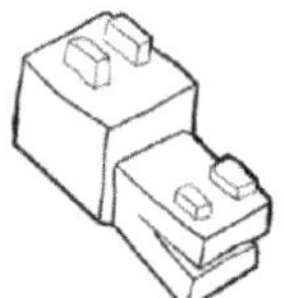

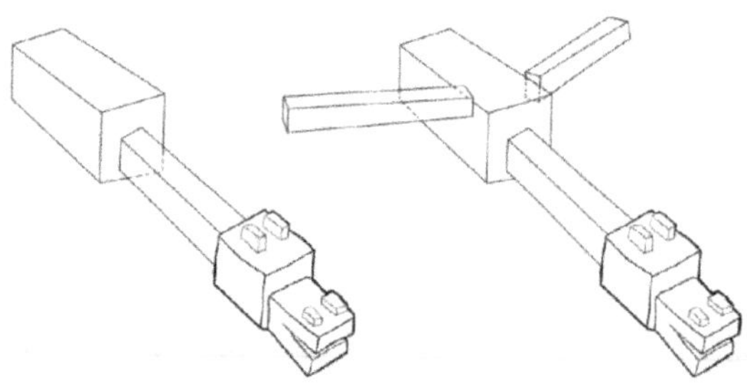

2 NOW WE CAN DRAW THE DRAGON'S TORSO. START BY DRAWING THE DRAGON'S LONG THIN NECK AND THEN DRAW A LARGE CUBOID FOR ITS BODY. THEN DRAW TWO SMALLER AND THINNER CUBOIDS ON THE SIDES OF THE TORSO TO START OF ITS WINGS.

3 EXTEND WING BASE BY ADDING THINNER CUBOIDS.

4 NEXT STEP, DRAW THE DRAGON'S TAIL.

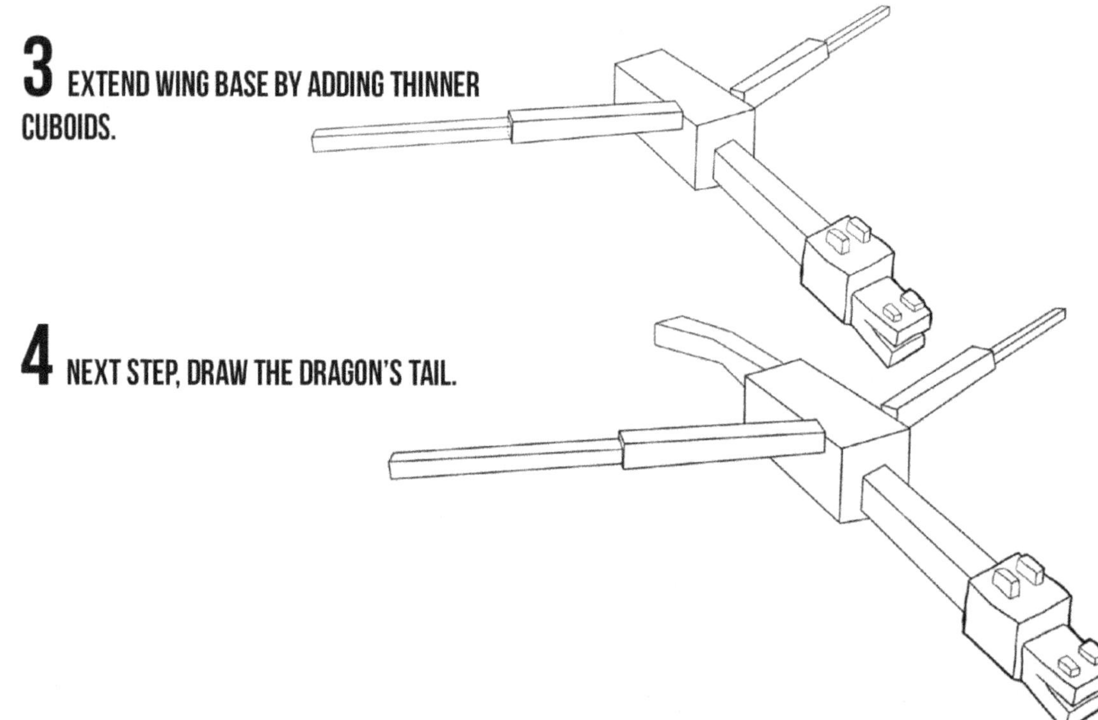

DRAGON

5 DRAW CURVE AND STRAIGHT LINES ON THE DRAGON'S WINGS TO MAKE IT APPEAR LIKE IT IS FLYING.

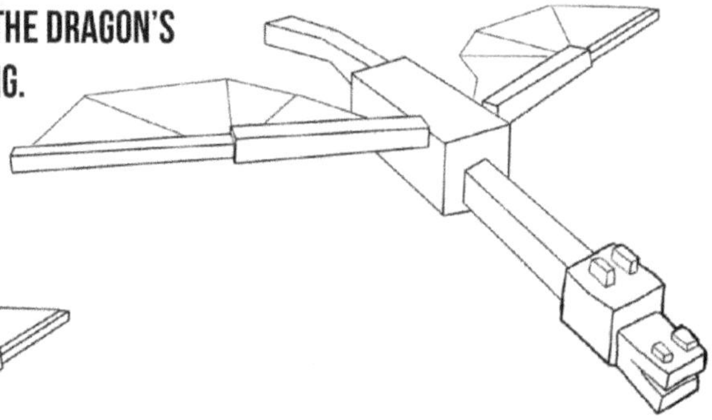

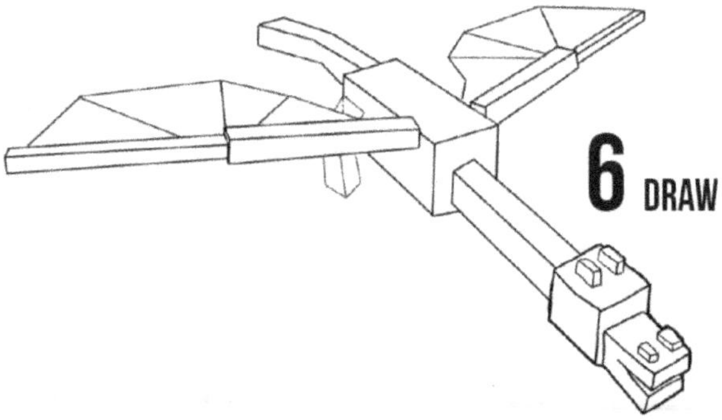

6 DRAW THE LEG OF THE DRAGON AS SHOWN IN THIS STEP.

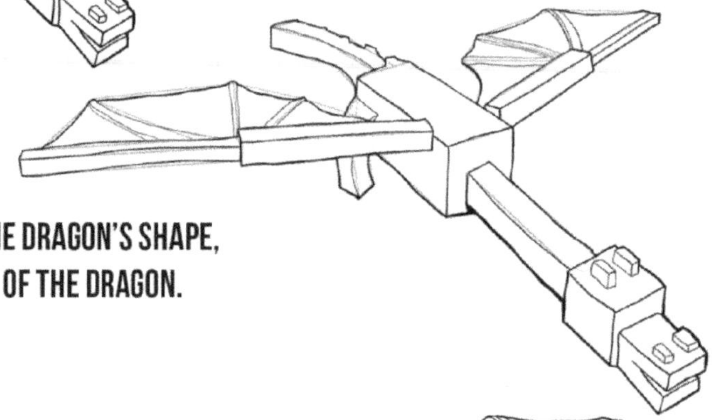

7 NOW THAT WE HAVE COMPLETED THE DRAGON'S SHAPE, USE THICK LINES TO OUTLINE THE BODY OF THE DRAGON.

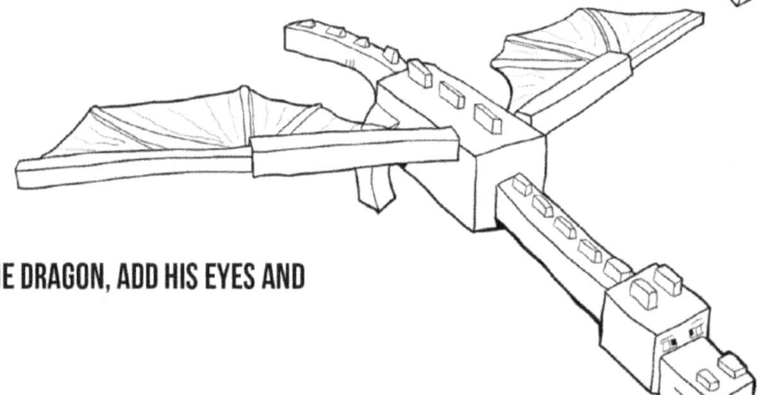

8 TO FINISH DRAWING THE DRAGON, ADD HIS EYES AND SPINES ON ITS BACK.

BAT

1 START BY DRAWING TWO IRREGULAR SQUARES, WITH THE SMALLER SQUARE ON THE UPPER LEFT PART.
NEXT STEP FOLLOW THE FULL LINE AS SHOWN IN THE IMAGE AND ERASE THE DOTTED LINE. ADD ITS EARS AND TRACE THE OUTLINE OF THE HEAD WITH THICKER LINES.

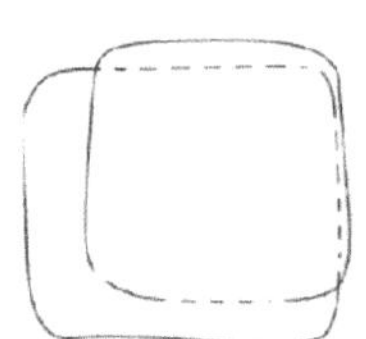

2 THE NEXT STEP IS TO DRAW A RECTANGULAR PRISM FOR ITS BODY. MAKE SURE THAT THERE'S A LITTLE SPACE IN BETWEEN THE HEAD AND THE BODY TO MAKE IT APPEAR THAT THE HEAD IS PIVOTED. ADD HIS WINGS NEXT.

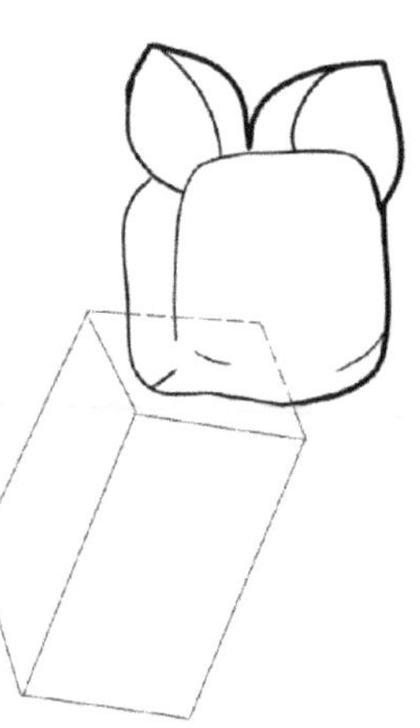
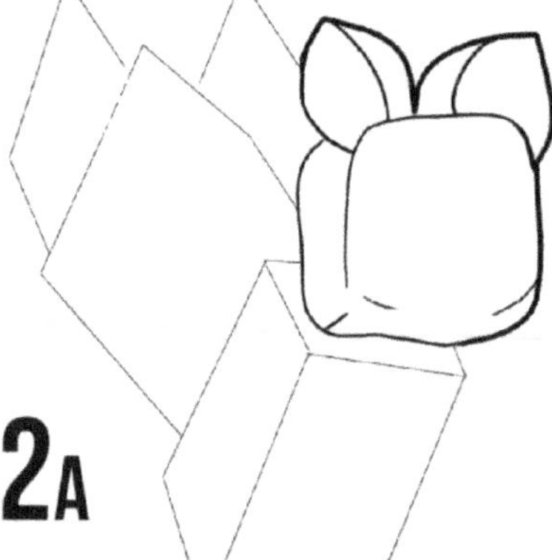

3 ALMOST DONE! USE THICKER LINES TO OUTLINE ITS BODY. IN STEP 3A, DRAW HIS EYES, NOSE, TEETH, AND FEET WITH CLAWS.

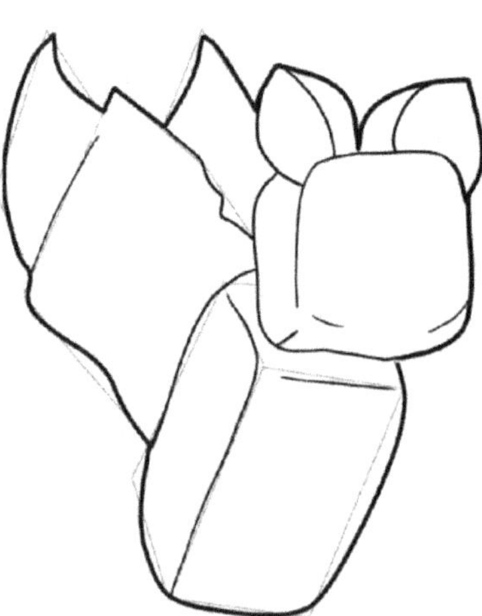

ENDER GUARDIAN

1 THIS STEP IS REALLY EASY! LET'S START WITH A LARGE CUBE.

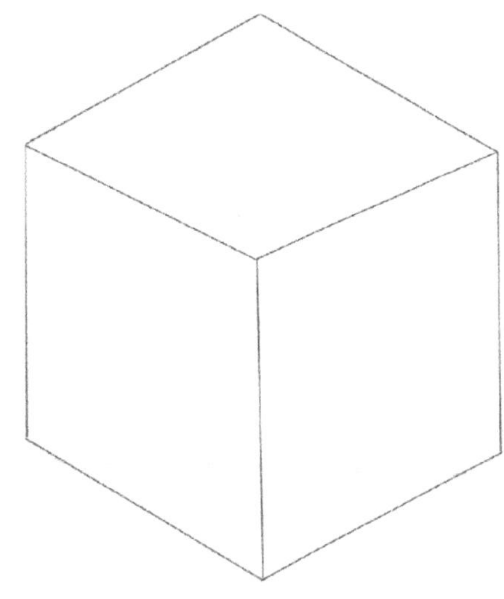

2 NOW DRAW TWO SQUARES ON THE CUBE AS SHOWN IN THIS IMAGE

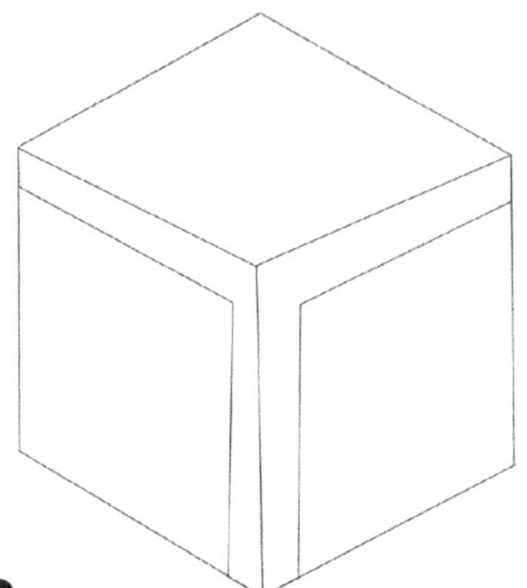

3 FOLLOW THIS DRAWING TO MAKE A SMALL SQUARE ON THE FRONT BOTTOM CORNER, AND FORM TWO RECTANGLES FACING INSIDE. YOU CAN ERASE DOTTED LINES.

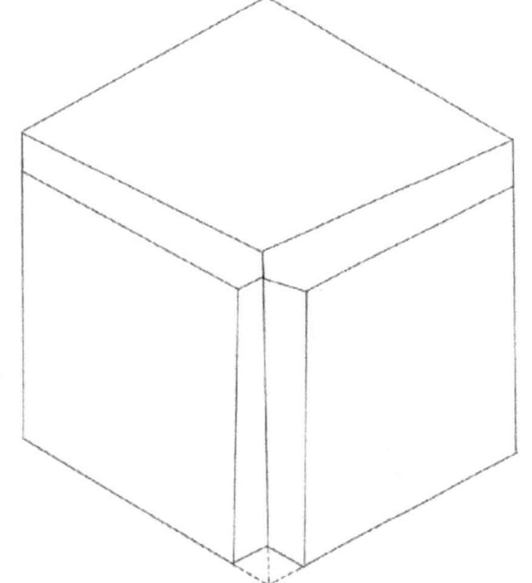

4 THIS LOOKS COMPLICATED BUT IT IS REALLY EASY JUST FOLLOW THE ILLUSTRATION SHOWN ABOVE.

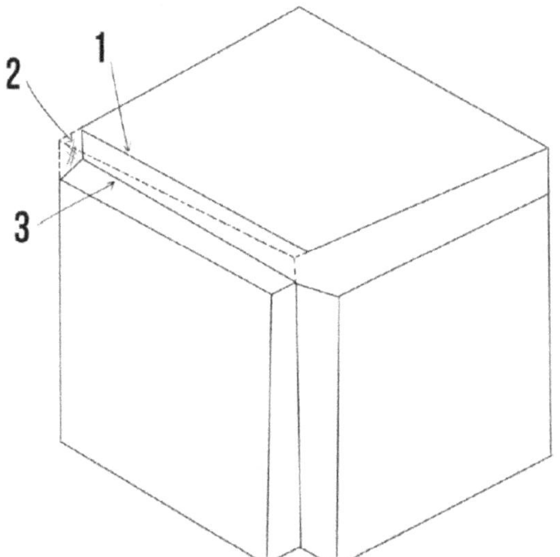

ENDER GUARDIAN

DIFFICULTY LEVEL

5 LET'S CONECT MARKED CORNERS. AFTER THAT, DRAW A PARALLEL LINE STARTING FROM LOWER MARKED CORNER. TO FINISH THIS STEP, ADD SHORT LINE TO FINISH YOUR SIDE.

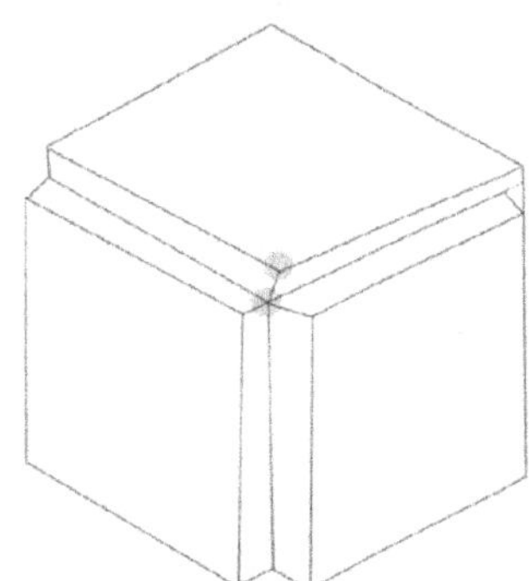

6 NOW THAT WE HAVE SHAPED HER BODY, LET'S DRAW HER TAIL.

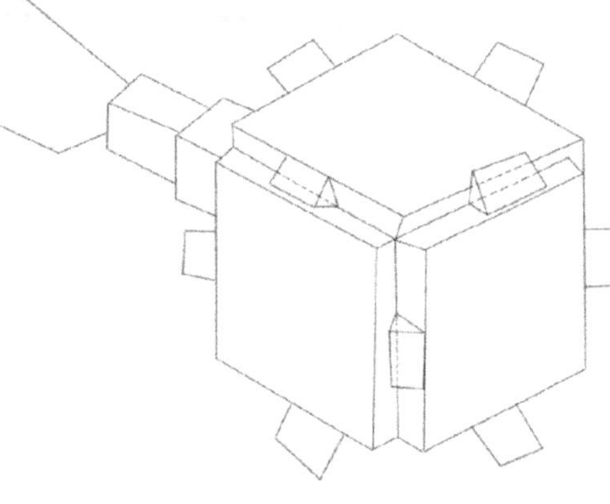

7 ALMOST DONE. ALL SHE NEEDS IS HER SPIKES, SO, DRAW A FUTURE SHAPE OF HER SCARY SPIKES JUST LIKE IN OUR SCHEME.

8 TO FINISH IT, JUST FOLLOW THE GUIDE AND USE THICKER LINES TO FORM ITS FINAL BODY. DRAW ITS FACE AND SOME DETAILS WHICH WILL MAKE THIS GUARDIAN SUPER COOL!

BREWING STAND

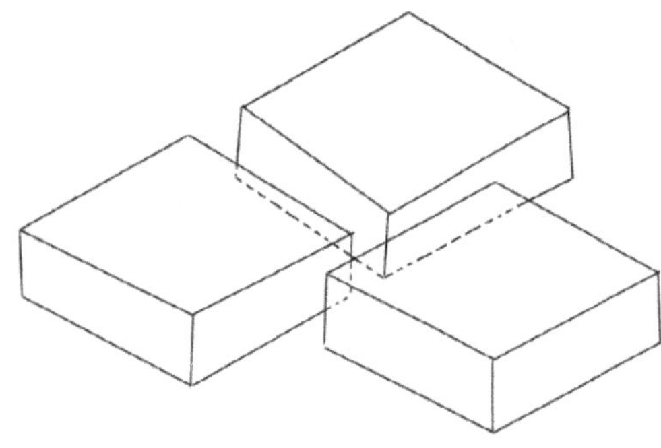

1 FIRST, DRAW THREE SEPARATE CUBES ADJACENT TO ONE ANOTHER, AND THIS IS GOING TO BE THE BASE OF OUR BREWING STAND. ERASE DOTTED LINES.

2 DRAW A VERTICAL RECTANGULAR PRISM AT THE MIDDLE OF THE BASE OF THE BREWING STAND.

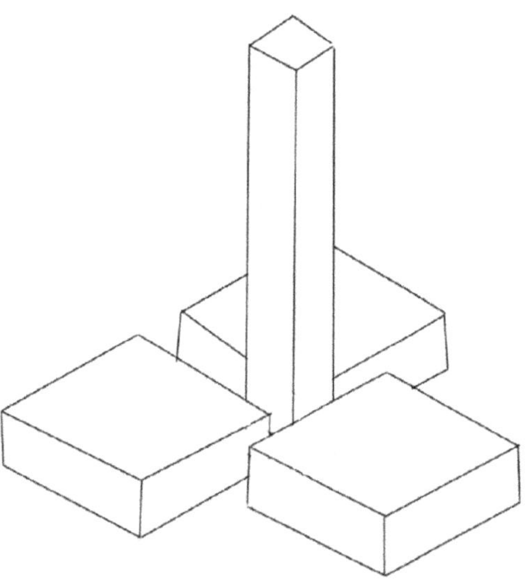

3 THIS IS WHAT IT SHOULD LOOK LIKE WHEN YOU ERASE ALL DOTTED LINES IN STEP 2.

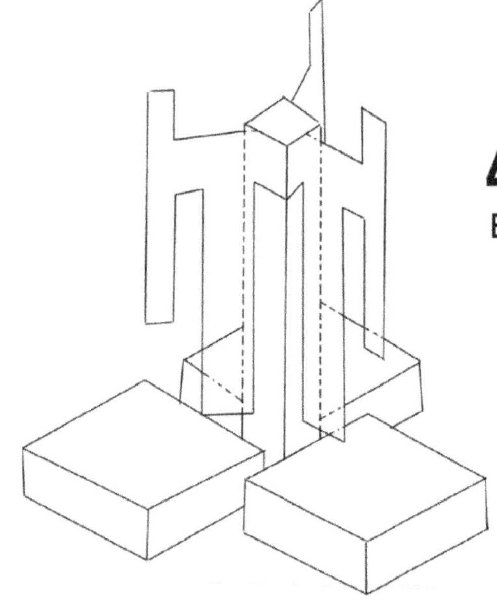

4 FOLLOW THIS DRAWING TO FORM THE SIDES OF THE BREWING STAND.

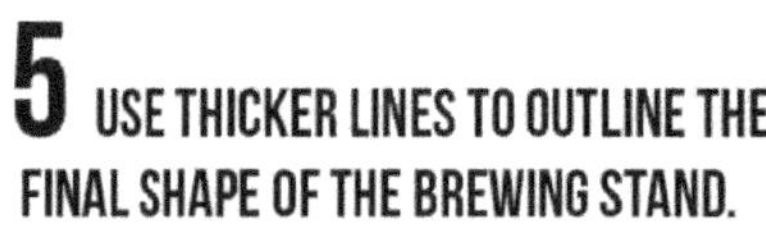

5 USE THICKER LINES TO OUTLINE THE FINAL SHAPE OF THE BREWING STAND.

6 ADD SOME FINISHING DETAILS AND IT IS DONE!

ENDERMITE

1 TO DRAW AN ENDERMITE, START WITH A CUBOID, AND DRAW ANOTHER BIGGER ONE BEHIND IT. NEXT DRAW TWO MORE CUBOIDS WITH THE THIRD CUBOID BEING THE LARGEST OF THE FOUR CUBOIDS JUST LIKE IN DRAWING 1A.

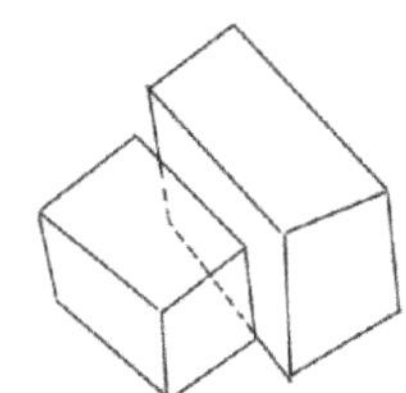

1A

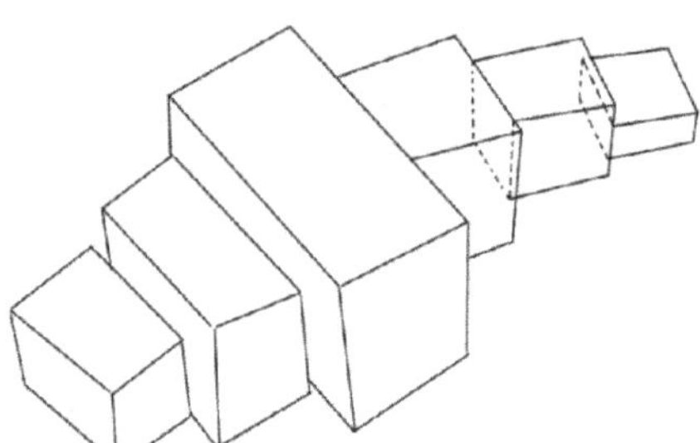

2 CONTINUE STACKING MORE CUBOIDS IN DESCENDING SIZES TO GET THE FINAL SHAPE OF THE ENDERMITES.

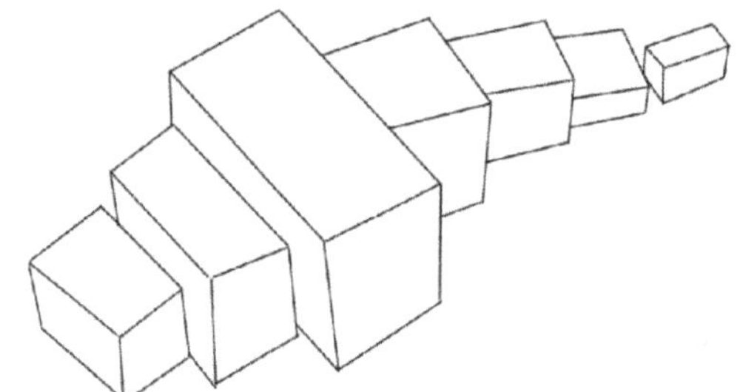

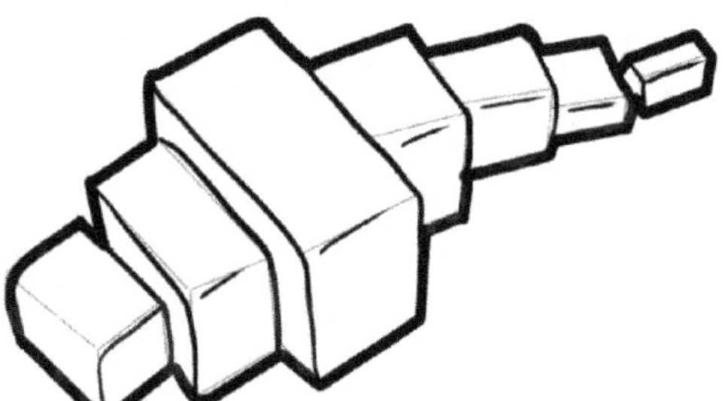

3 FINALLY, USE THICKER LINES TO OUTLINE THE FINAL SHAPE OF THE ENDERMITES, ADD ITS EYES AND SOME SHADINGS.

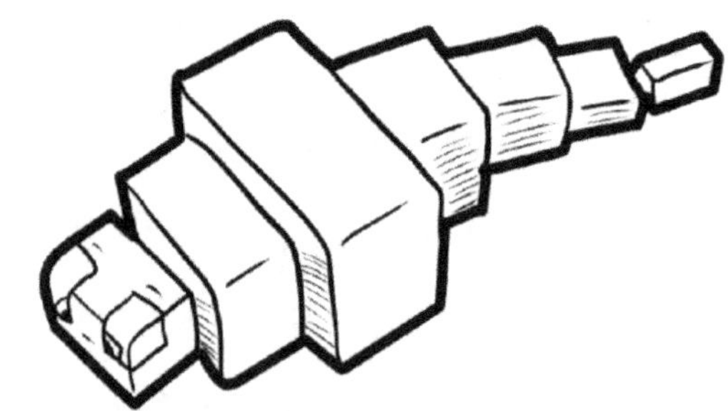

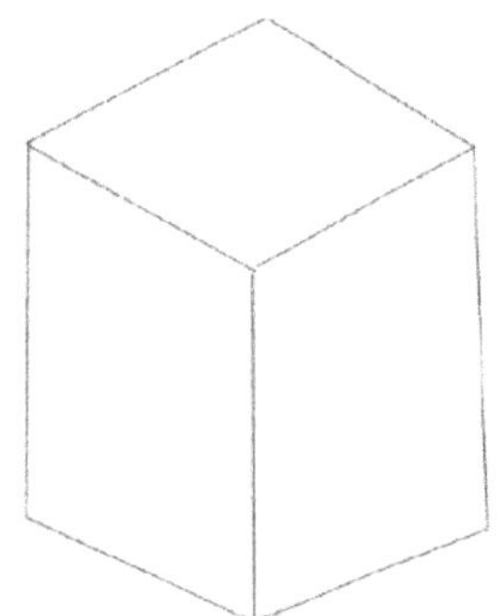

1 START WITH THIS SHAPE FOR HIS HEAD.

2 DRAW HIM A NOSE.

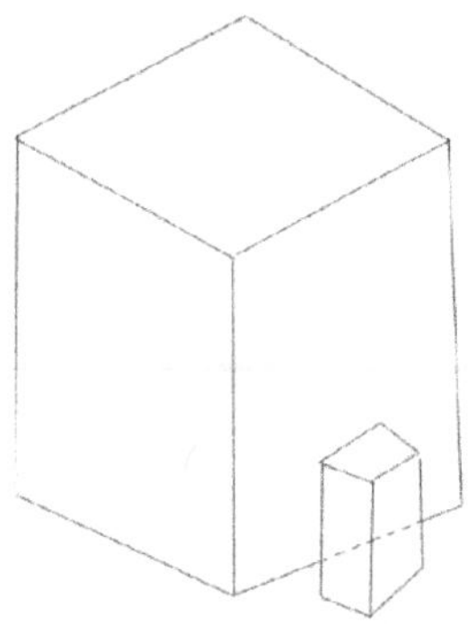

3 DRAW A RECTANGULAR PRISM BELOW HIS HEAD.

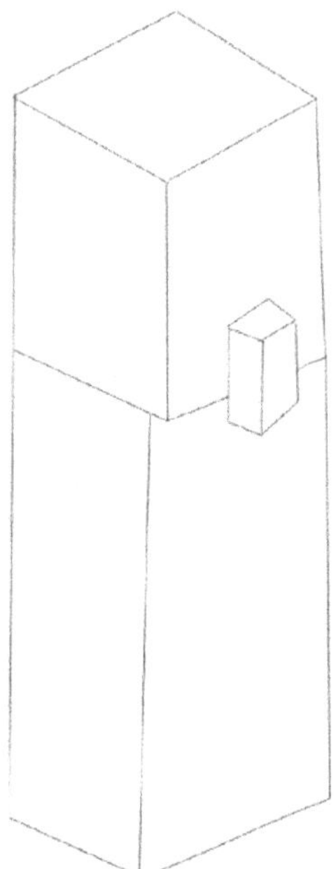

DIFFICULTY LEVEL

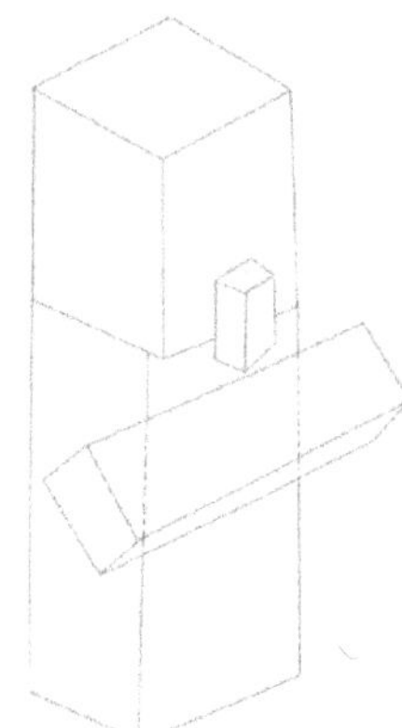

4 DRAW A HORIZONTAL RECTANGULAR PRISM ACROSS THE UPPER PART OF HIS TORSO.

5 NEXT, DRAW HIS SHOULDER AS SHOWN IN THIS STEP.

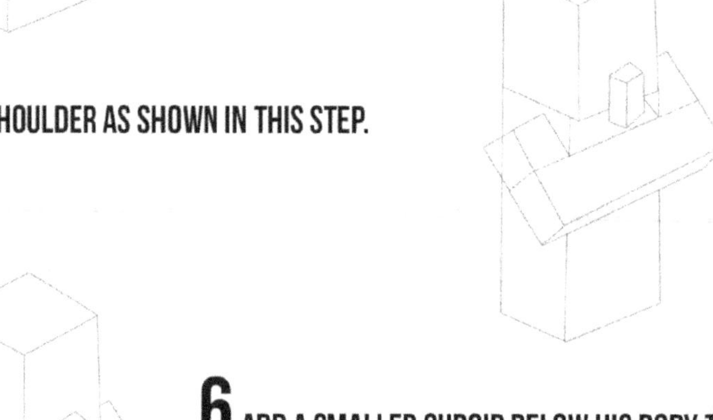

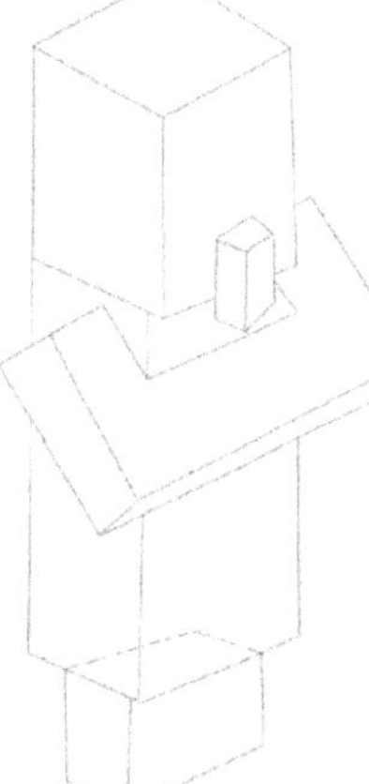

6 ADD A SMALLER CUBOID BELOW HIS BODY TO MAKE HIS FEET AND REMOVE ALL LINE GUIDES.

7 NOW YOU CAN TRACE WITH THICKER LINES HIS FINAL SHAPE. DRAW HIS FACE AND DETAILS ON HIS CLOTHING.

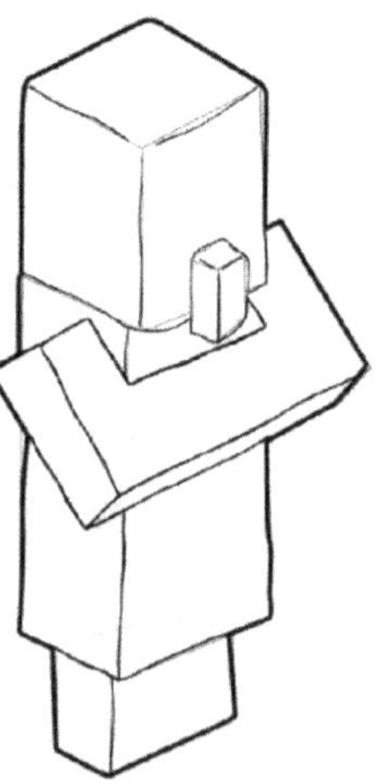

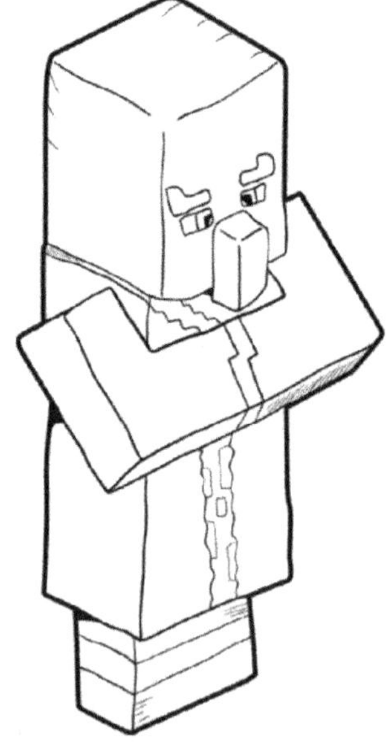

HORSE

1 START WITH THIS BIG CUBOID TO FORM ITS TORSO. AFTER THAT DRAW THE SECOND SHAPE AS SHOWN IN THE SECOND ILLUSTRATION. PAY ATTENTION TO THE MARKED BROKEN LINES, YOU WILL NEED THEM IN THE NEXT STEP.

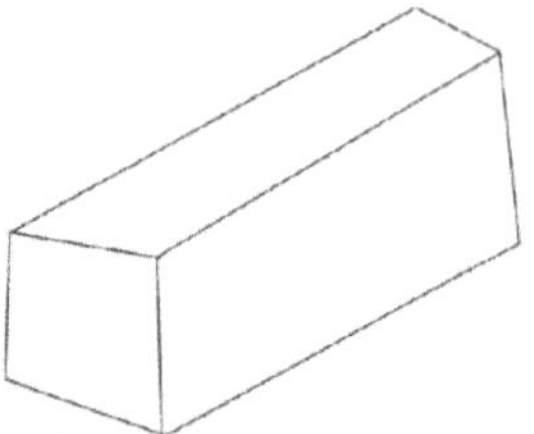 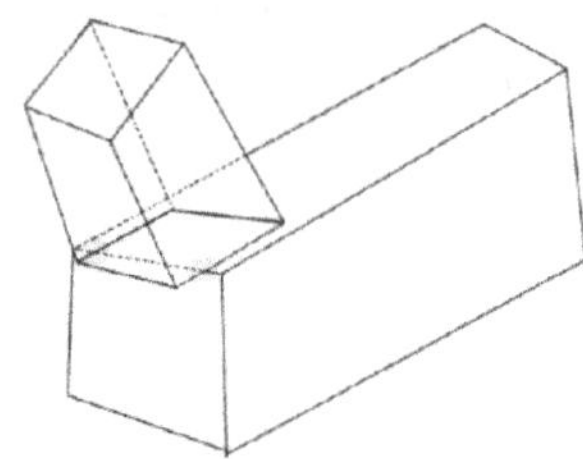

2 USE THE LINES FROM THE UPPER SHAPE AND EXTEND THEM A BIT LIKE WE MARKED IT. DRAW PARALLEL LINES FROM THE MARKED CORNERS, AND STOP WHEN YOU REACHED YOUR EXTENDED LINE. THE SECOND DRAWING SHOWS THE SHAPE OF THE HORSE WE ARE AIMING FOR. ADD THE EARS OF THE HORSE AFTER YOU FINISH DRAWING THE SHAPE OF ITS BODY.

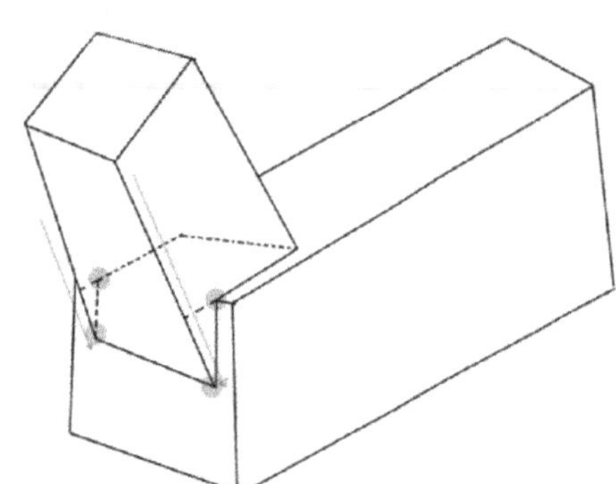 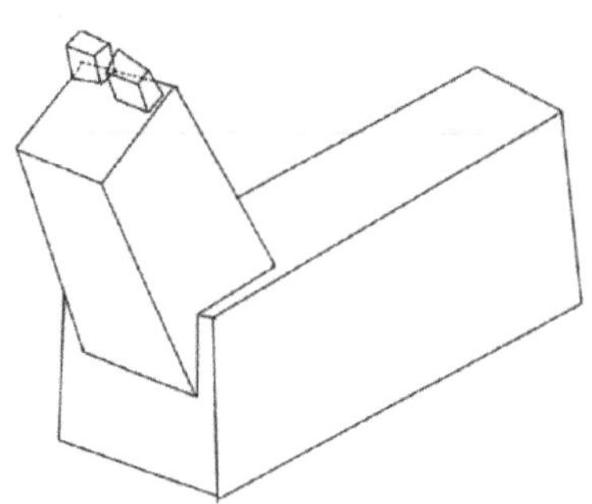

3 ADD ITS SNOUT FOLLOWING THE SHAPE SHOWN IN THE IMAGE BELOW.

4 DRAW ITS LEGS NEXT.

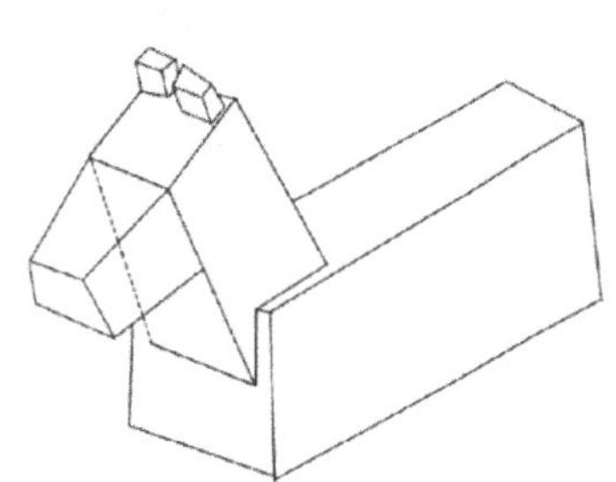 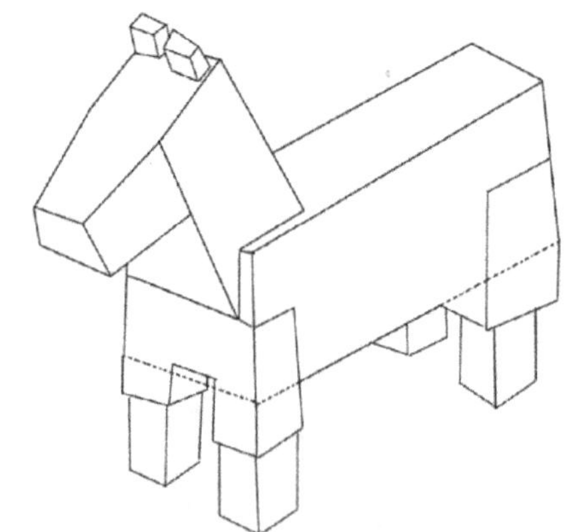

HORSE

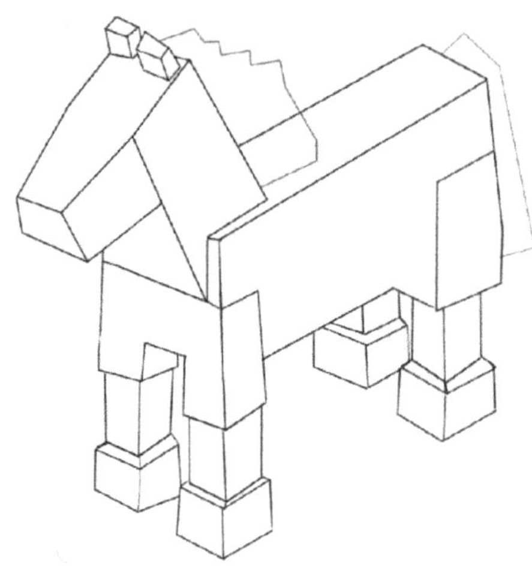

5 ADD FOUR CUBES BELOW ITS LEGS TO CREATE ITS HOOFS. DRAW ITS TAIL AS WELL.

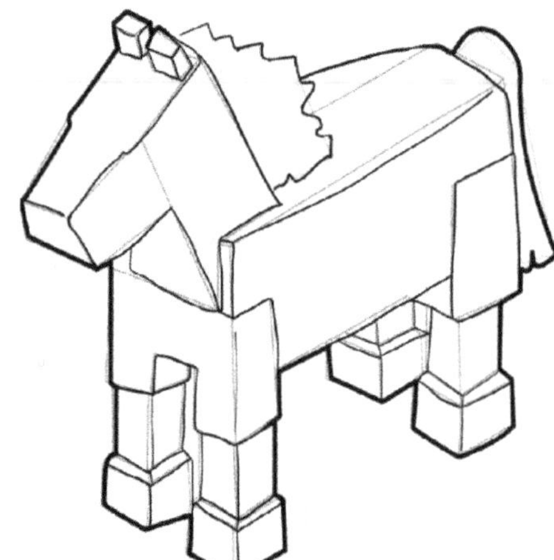

6 TRACE THE OUTLINE OF THE HORSE WITH THICKER LINES TO FORM THE FINAL SHAPE OF THE HORSE

7 NOW FINISH DRAWING YOUR HORSE BY ADDING ITS EYES AND DRAWING ITS THICK MANE.

INFINITE FIRE

1 START WITH THIS SHAPE:

2 NOW, DRAW A FLAME AND A SIDE OF THE BOWL WHICH HOLDS AN INFINITE FIRE.

3 DRAW THE FLAME AND THE SIDE OF THE BOWL WHICH HOLDS THE FIRE.

 CHICKEN

1 LET'S DRAW THIS CHICKEN. START WITH THE BODY — A LARGE CUBE. THEN LIKE IN IMAGE 1A DRAW A RECTANGLE ABOVE THE CUBE. THEN ADD A DIMENSION TO THE RECTANGLE TO MAKE IT LOOK LIKE A PRISM.

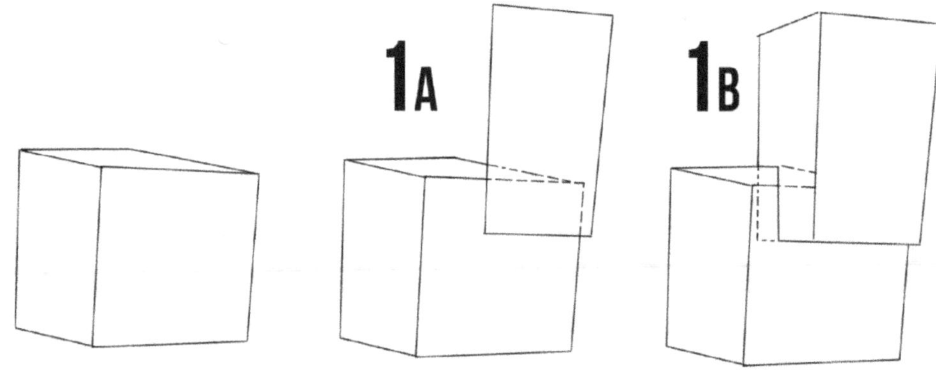

2 DRAW THE CHICKEN'S WING, FOLLOWED BY ITS BEAK AND FINALLY ITS WADDLE.

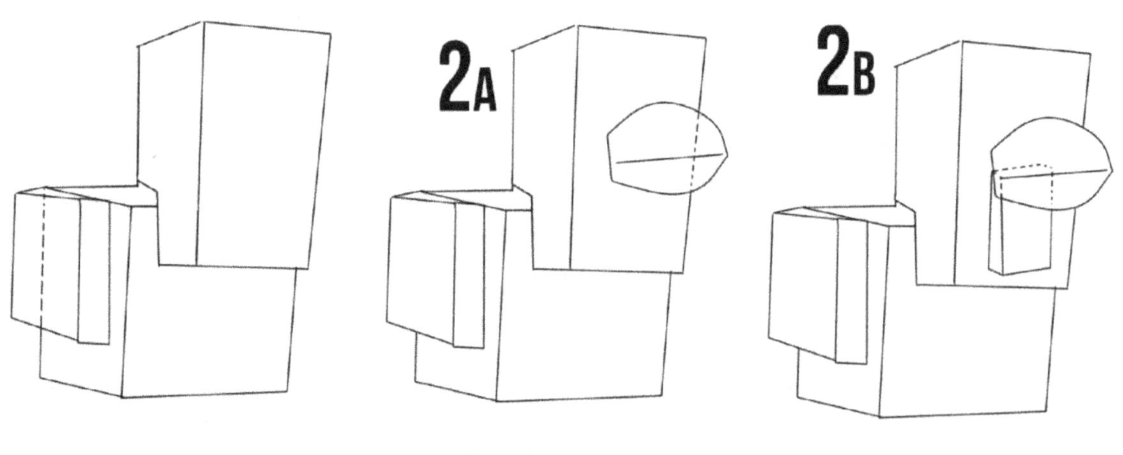

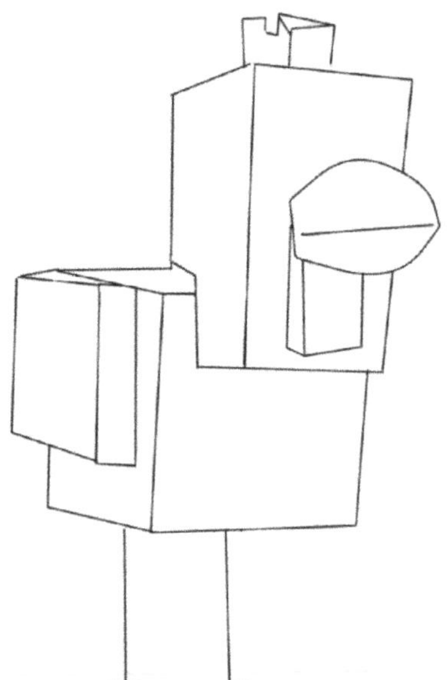

3 DRAW TWO LINE GUIDES FOR THE CHICKEN'S LEGS AND DRAW ITS TALON TOO.

4 DRAW ITS LEGS AND FEET. FOLLOW THE GUIDELINES AND DRAW FINAL SHAPE OF CHICKEN.

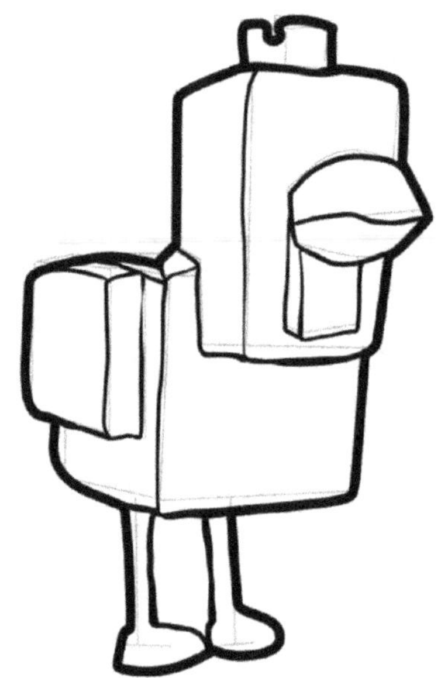

5 FINALLY, DRAW THE CHICKEN'S EYES AND ADD SOME SHADING.

ENDERMAN

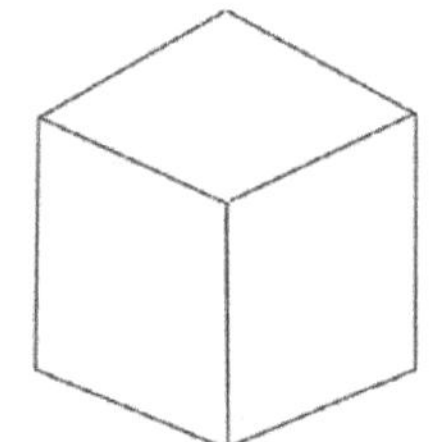

1 START BY DRAWING A CUBE FOR THE ENDERMAN'S HEAD.

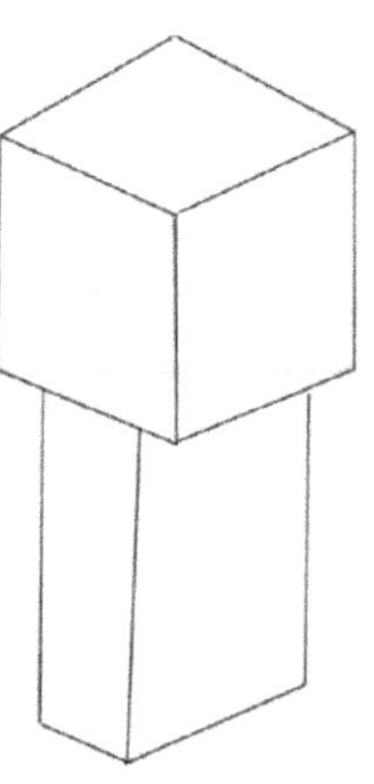

2 DRAW A RECTANGULAR PRISM BELOW THE ENDERMAN'S HEAD TO CREATE ITS TORSO.

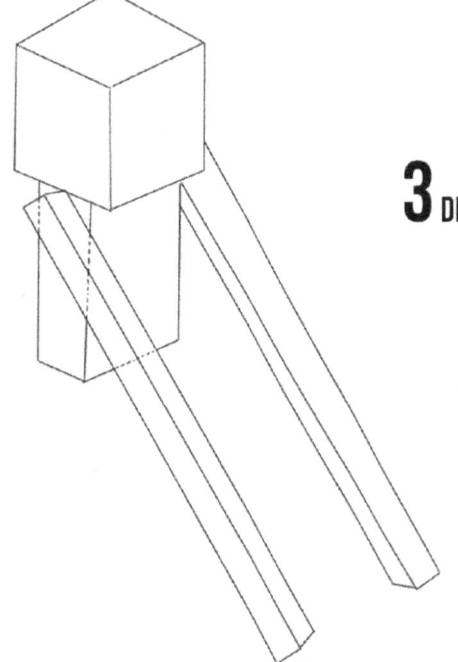

3 DRAW HIS LONG ARMS AS SHOWN IN THE IMAGE.

ENDERMAN

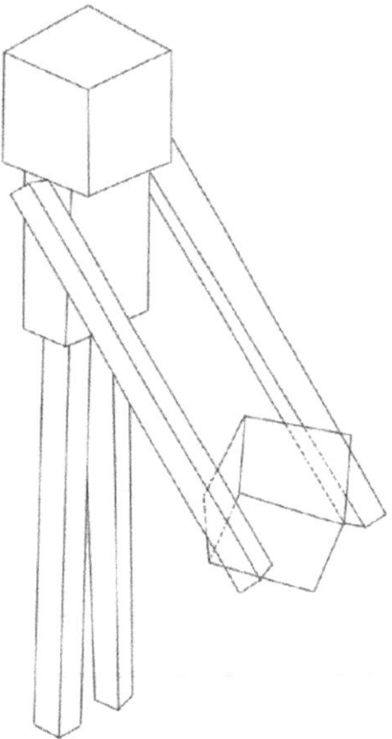

4 NOW – DRAW THE ENDERMAN'S LONG SLENDER LEGS AND A BLOCK IN BETWEEN HIS ARMS.

5 ALMOST DONE! TRACE WITH THICKER LINES THE OUTLINE OF THE ENDERMAN'S BODY AND THE BLOCK HE IS HOLDING.

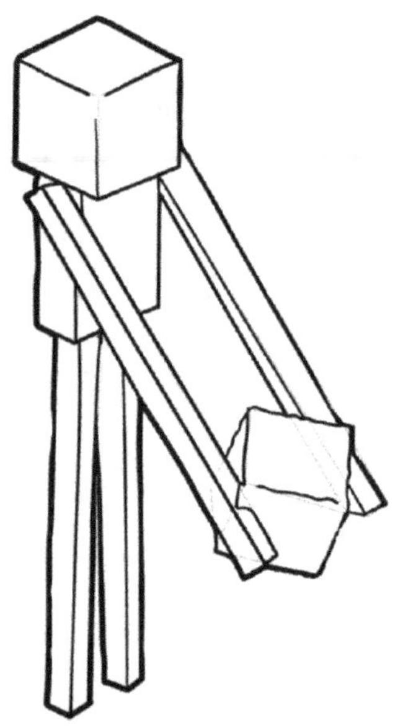

6 TO FINISH YOUR ENDERMAN, DRAW HIM A FACE. SHADINGS AND ADDITIONAL DETAILS WILL MAKE HIM REALLY COOL.

GHAST

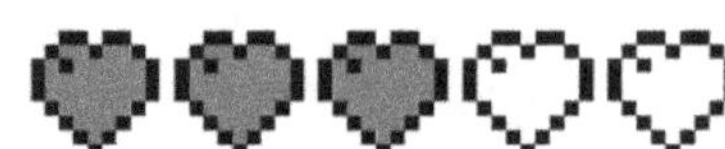

DIFFICULTY LEVEL

1 TO DRAW A GHAST, FOLLOW THESE STEPS. FIRST, DRAW A CUBE, AFTER THAT DRAW SMALL RECTANGLES FOR ITS LEGS.

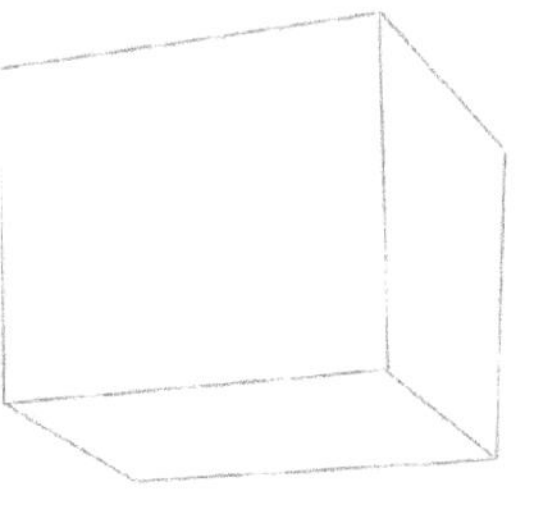

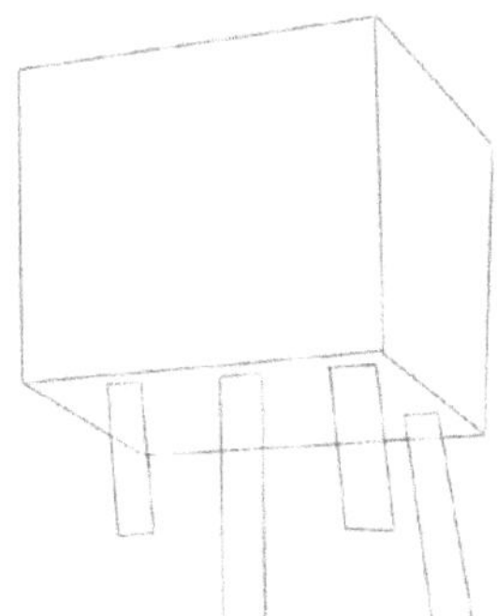

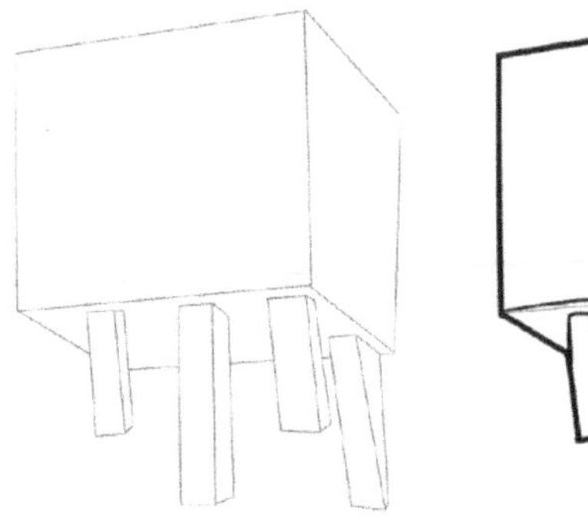

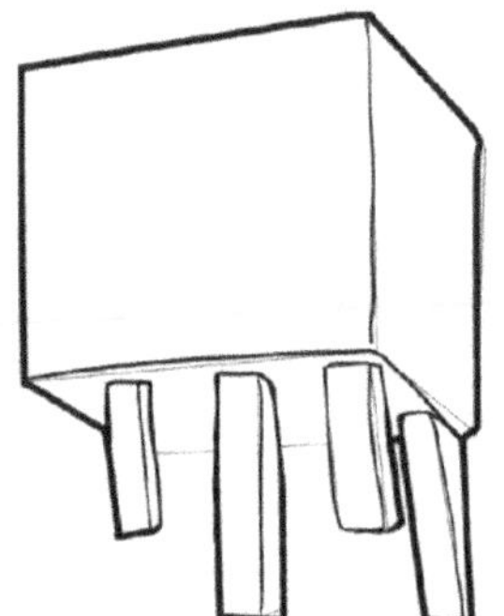

2 MAKE HIS LEGS REALISTIC BY DRAWING ITS SIDES JUST LIKE IN THE LEFT PICTURE.

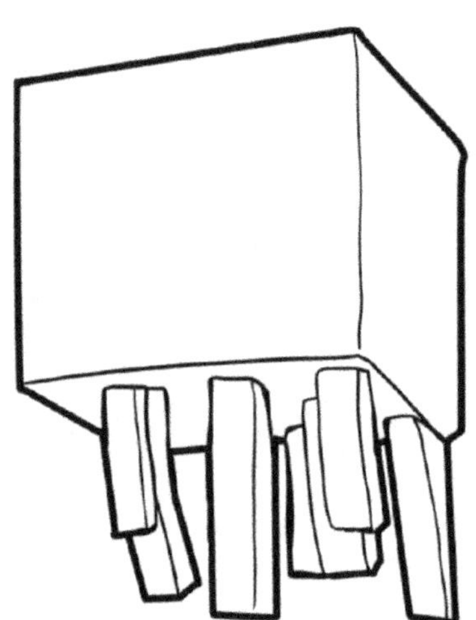

3 LET'S DRAW THIS GHAST EVEN MORE LEGS AND USE THICKER LINES TO TRACE THE FINAL SHAPE OF THE GHAST AND ITS LEGS.

4 TO FINISH IT, JUST DRAW IT A FACE AND SOME LINES FOR SHADING. COOL, ISN'T IT?

IRON GOLEM

1 DRAW THE SHAPE OF ITS HEAD BY FOLLOWING THE ILLUSTRATIONS BELOW.

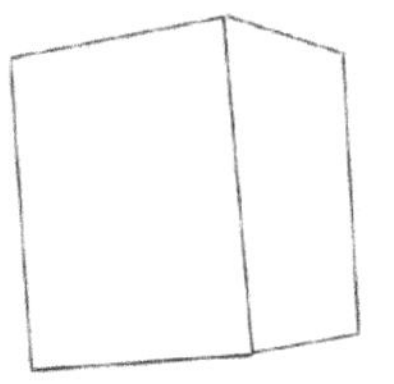 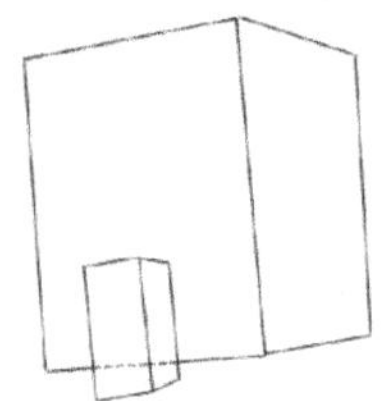 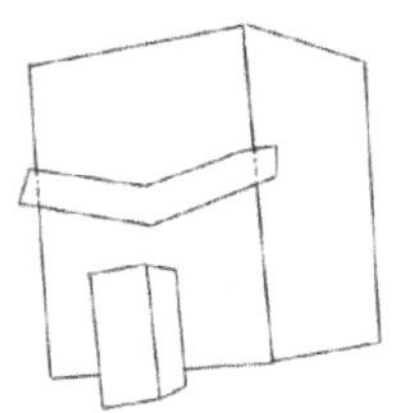

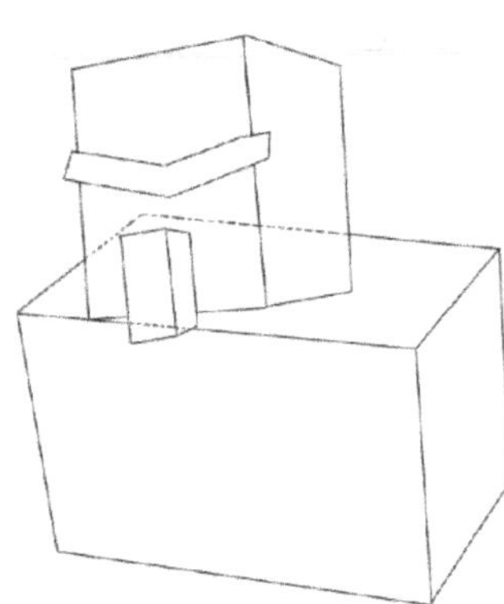

2 DRAW HIM A TORSO. IT IS JUST A BIG CUBOID. ERASE ALL DOTTED LINES.

3 NOW HANDS! START WITH ITS SHOULDERS, AND DRAW TWO LONG RECTANGLES ON ITS SIDES.

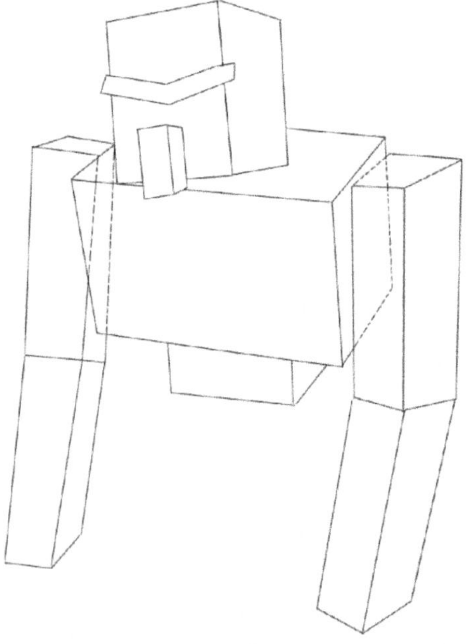

IRON GOLEM

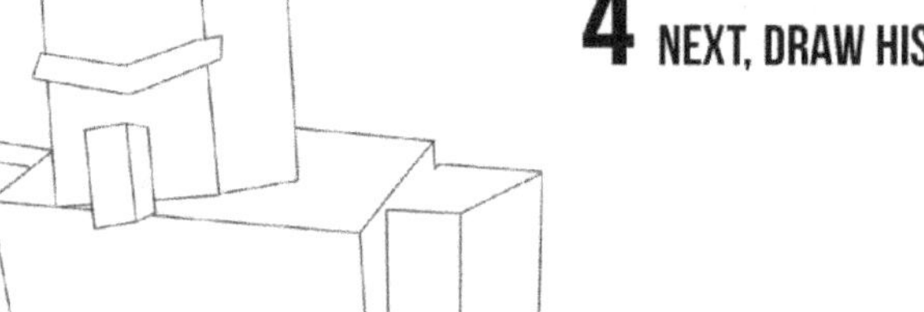

4 NEXT, DRAW HIS LEGS AND THE LOWER PART OF HIS TORSO.

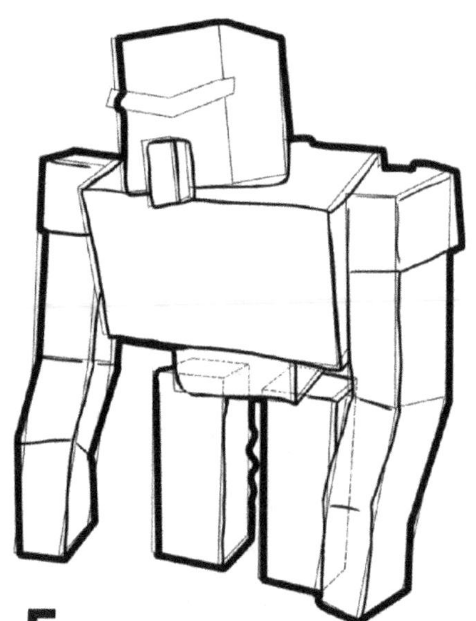

5 ALMOST DONE! USE THICKER LINES TO DRAW HIS FINAL SHAPE, AND ERASE GUIDELINES AFTER THAT.

6 TO FINISH DRAWING THIS IRON GOLEM, DRAW THE REST OF HIS FACE. DRAW VINES ALL OVER ITS BODY AS WELL.

LLAMA

1 LET'S START WITH A LARGE CUBOID AND THEN DRAW A SMALLER SQUARE IN FRONT OF THE LARGE CUBOID AS SHOWN IN THE DRAWING TO THE RIGHT.

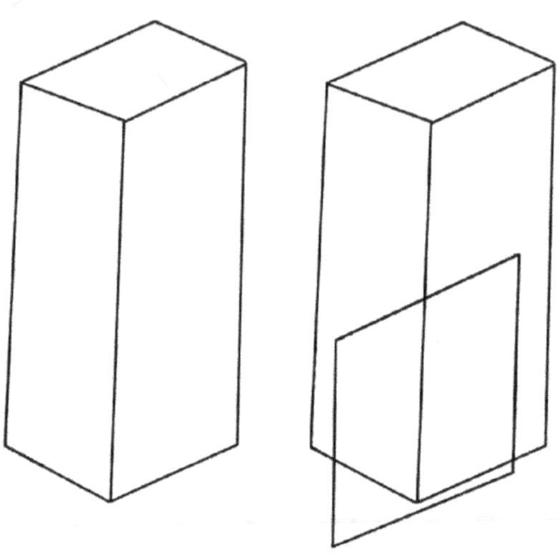

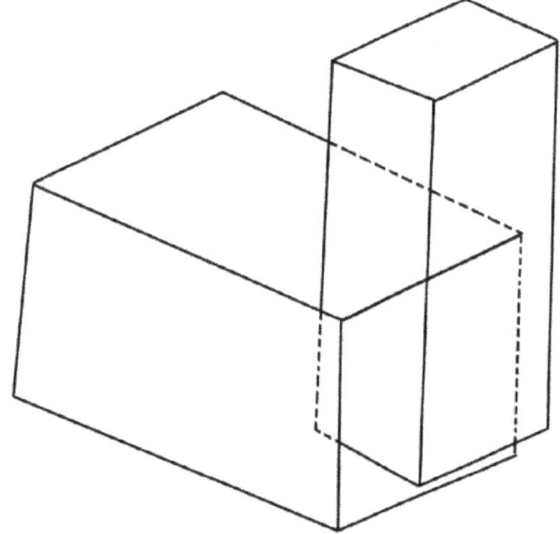

2 ADD DIMENSIONS TO THE SQUARE TO MAKE IT A RECTANGULAR PRISM. ERASE DOTTED LINES.

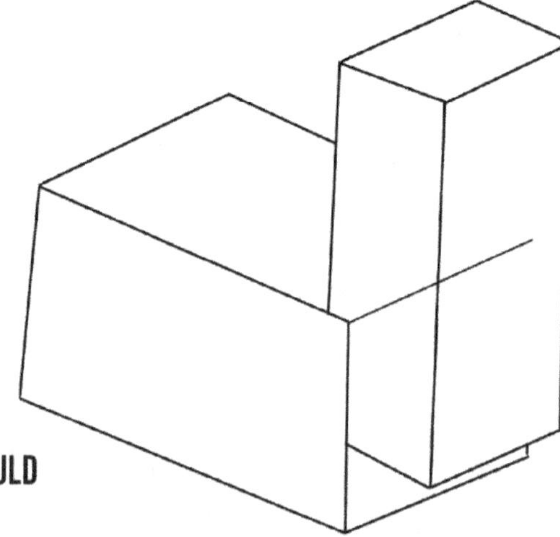

3 WHEN YOU ERASE GUIDELINES, YOU SHOULD HAVE A SHAPE LIKE THIS ONE.

LLAMA

DIFFICULTY LEVEL

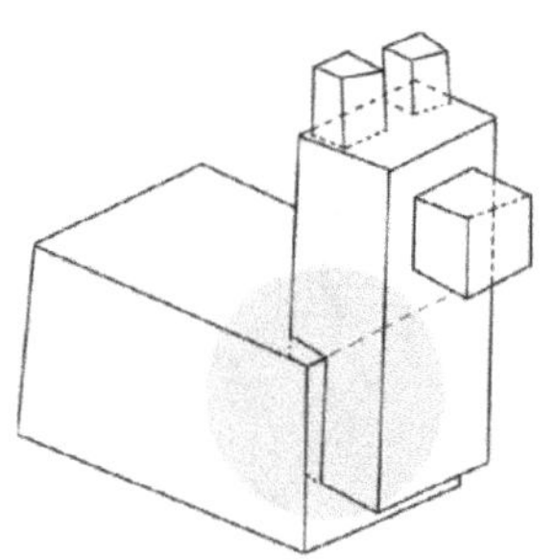

4 WE'RE ALMOST FINISHED DRAWING THE LLAMA'S BODY. DRAW THE EARS OF THE LLAMA FIRST AND HER MOUTH. AFTER THAT SEPARATE THE NECK FROM THE BODY AS SHOWN IN THE MARKED AREA.

5 DRAW THE LLAMA'S LEGS. ERASE ALL DOTTED LINES.

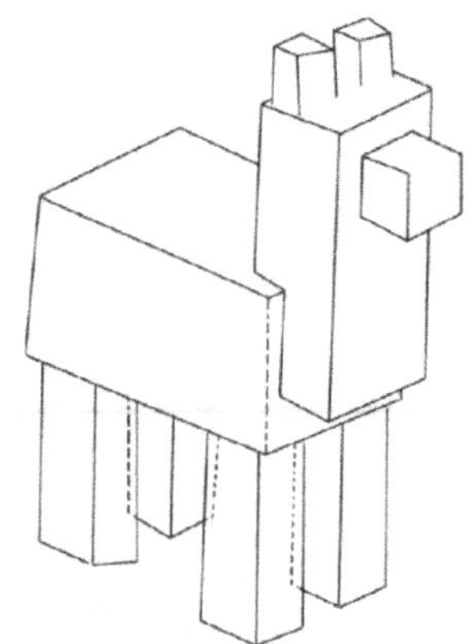

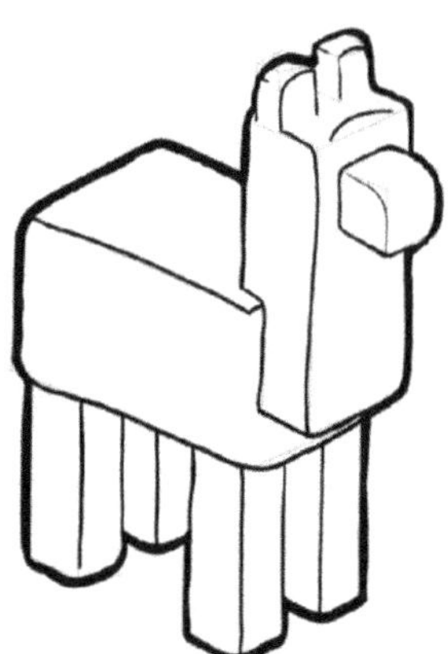

6 USE THICKER LINES TO TRACE THE FINAL SHAPE OF THE LLAMA'S BODY.

7 TO FINISH LLAMA, DRAW HER A CUTE FACE, FLUFFY TAIL AND MORE DETAILS JUST TO MAKE HER FUR LOOKS SUPER CURLY!

MAP

1 START WITH THIS SHAPE:

2 DRAW A SHAPE OF A ROLLED PAPER ON EACH SIDE.

3 ALMOST DONE! NOW YOU CAN FINISH YOUR MAP WITH SOME SMALL DETAILS ON THE SIDES, AND OF COURSE, DRAW ANY KIND OF SECRET TREASURE MAP!

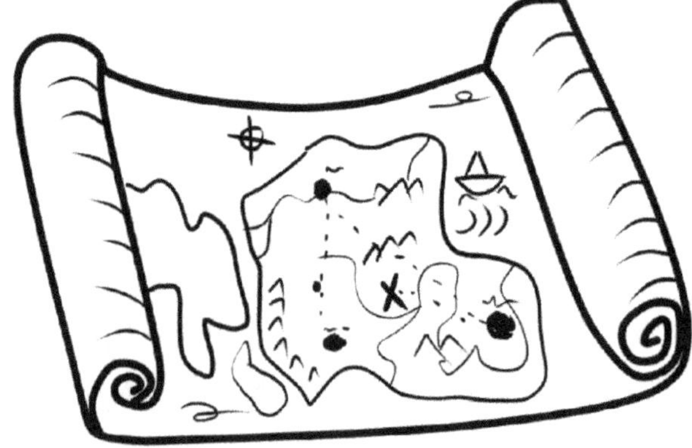

MOOSHROOM

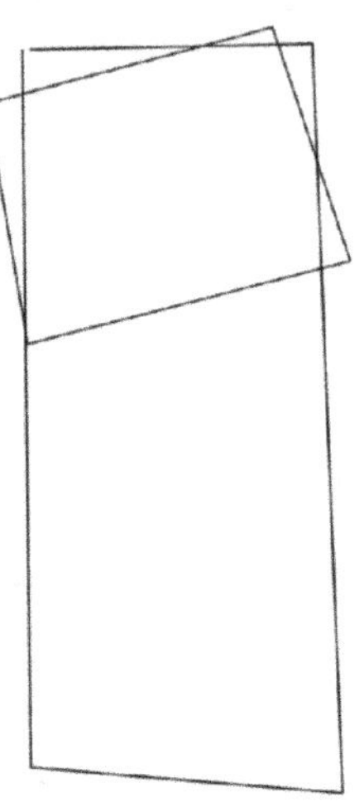

1 START BY DRAWING A SQUARE DRAWN OVER A VERTICAL RECTANGLE. THE SQUARE IS DRAWN ON AN ANGLE AND IS NOT PARALLEL TO THE RECTANGLE.

2 NOW, ON THE UPPER CORNER OF THE SQUARE DRAW THE MOOSHROOM'S HORNS AND ADD A HORIZONTAL RECTANGLE ACROSS THE LOWER PART OF THE SQUARE TO CREATE THE MOOSHROOM'S SNOUT.

3 DRAW THE MOOSHROOM'S HEAD AND BODY AND REMOVE GUIDELINES.

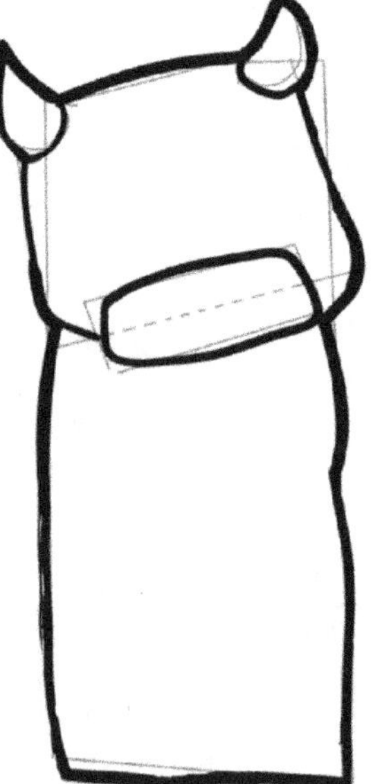

MOOSHROOM

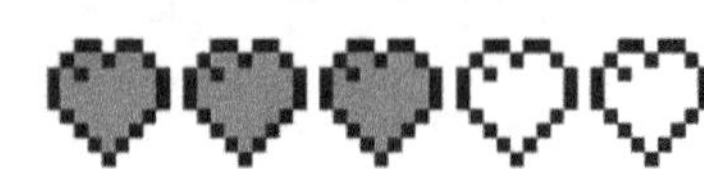

4 DRAW THE MOOSHROOM'S EARS BY DRAWING TWO TRIANGLES AT THE SIDE OF ITS FACE. DRAW THE LINES GUIDES FOR ITS FEET AS SHOWN IN THE IMAGE.

5 ALMOST DONE! USE THICKER LINES TO TRACE THE FINAL SHAPE OF HER BODY.

6 TO FINISH THIS DRAWING. DRAW HER EYES, SNOUT, CURLY TAIL AND OF COURSE MUSHROOMS ON HER BODY.

1 TO DRAW AN OCELOT'S HEAD, FOLLOW THESE STEPS: FIRST DRAW A CUBE. AFTER THAT ADD TWO MORE SMALL CUBES AND A RECTANGULAR PRISM TO FORM HIS EARS AND MOUTH.

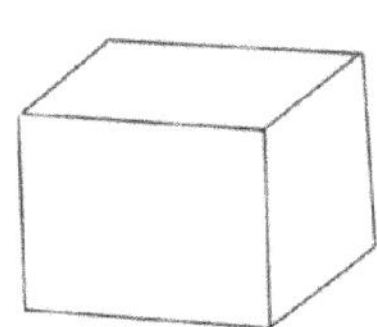
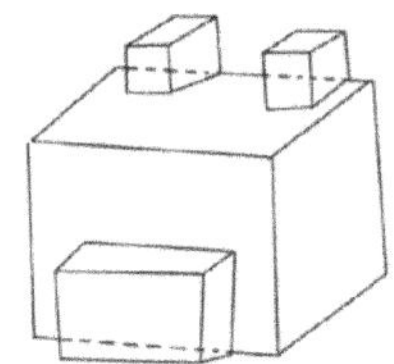
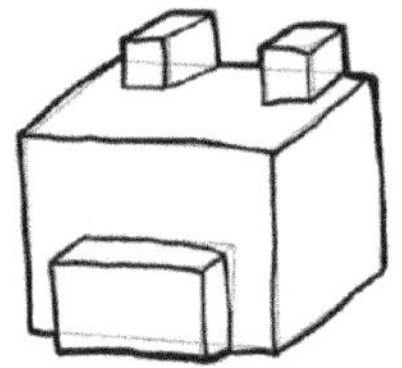

2 DRAW HIM A BODY BY FORMING A BIG CUBOID. ADD SMALL RECTANGLES TO FORM THE SHAPES OF HIS LEGS. FOLLOW THE NEXT ILLUSTRATIONS TO DRAW THE FINAL SHAPE OF HIS LEGS.

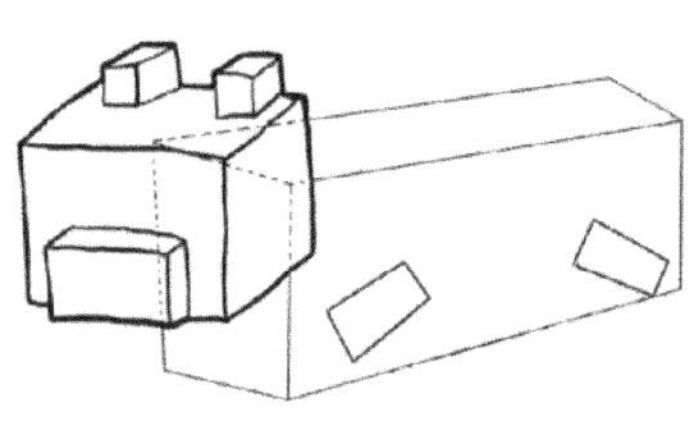
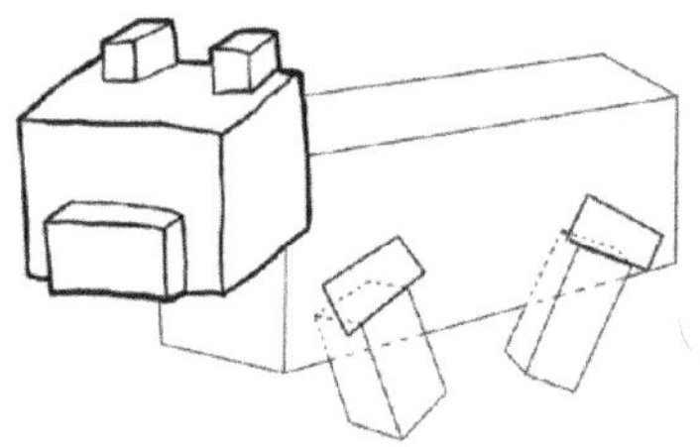
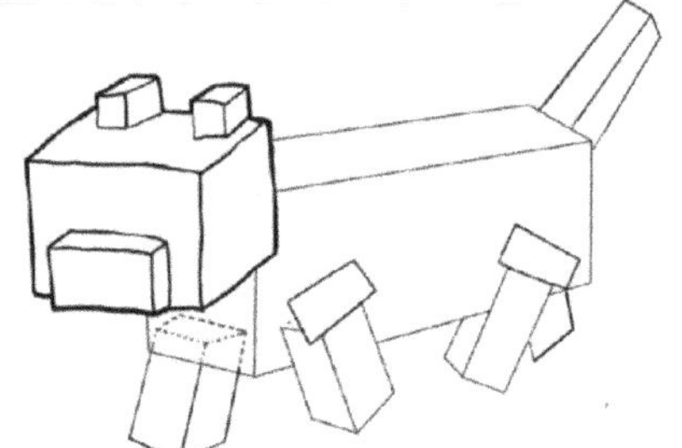

3 ALMOST DONE! NOW YOU CAN FINISH YOUR DRAWING WITH THICKER LINES FOR HIS FULL BODY SHAPE. AFTER THAT, ERASE GUIDELINES, ADD HIM A CUTE FACE AND A LOT OF STRIPES ON HIS FUR. ISN'T HE CUTE?

CARROT

1 START BY DRAWING THE SHAPE OF THE CARROT.

2 ADD ITS LEAVES.

3 TO FINISH IT, USE THINNER LINES TO DRAW WRINKLES ON ITS BODY AND SOME LINES TO SEPARATE ITS LEAVES.

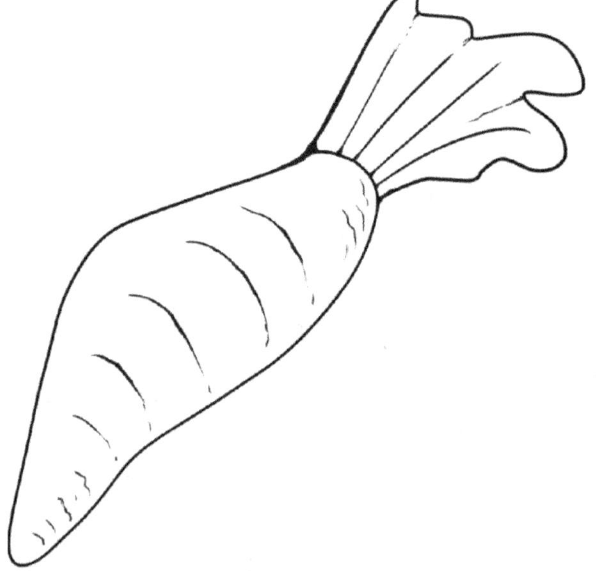

PARROT

1 TO DRAW A PARROT'S HEAD, FOLLOW THE ILLUSTRATIONS SHOWN BELOW. ERASE DOTTED LINES FOR THE NEXT STEP.
2.

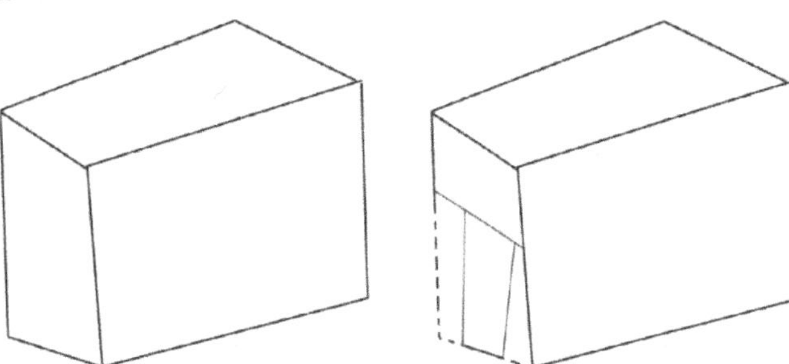

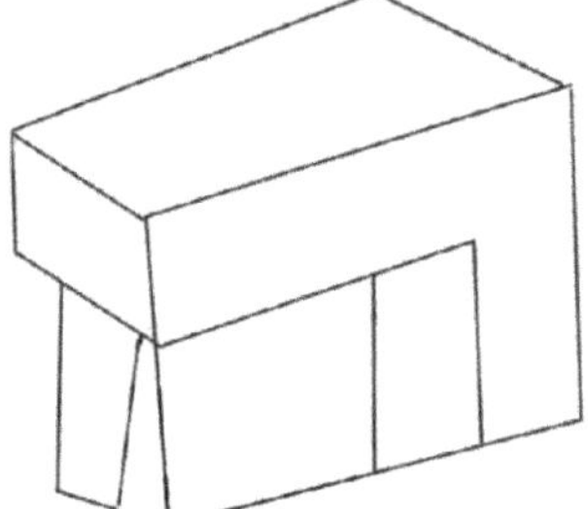

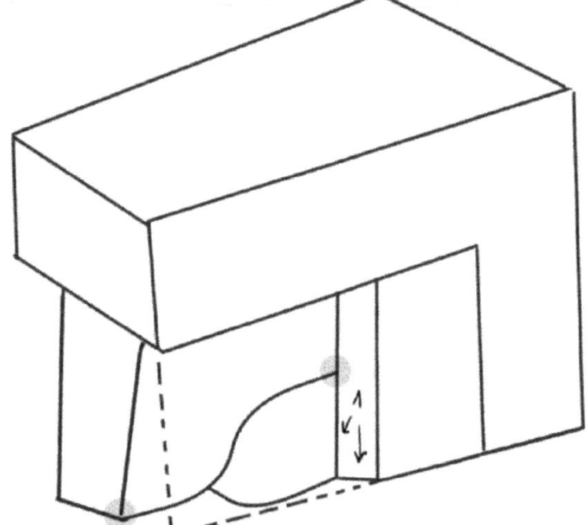

2 LET'S DRAW ITS BEAK! FIRST, FORM A SMALL TRAPEZOID FOLLOWING STEP 1. THAN DRAW A LINE FROM THE MARKED POINT. AND FOR THE LAST STEP DRAW THE LOWER PART OF THE BEAK.

3 NOW YOU CAN FINISH THE SHAPE OF ITS HEAD BY ADDING TALONS ON TOP OF IT.

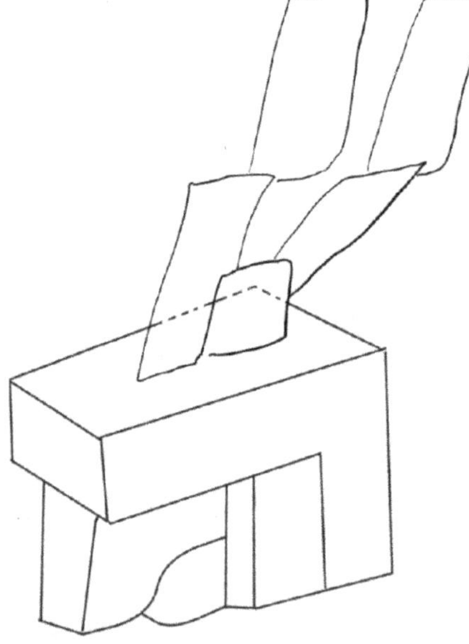

PARROT

4 LET'S DRAW THE REST OF THE BODY! START WITH A LARGE CUBOID FOR ITS BODY AND DRAW A RECTANGLE FOR ITS WINGS. DRAW THE LINE GUIDES FOR ITS FEET AS WELL.

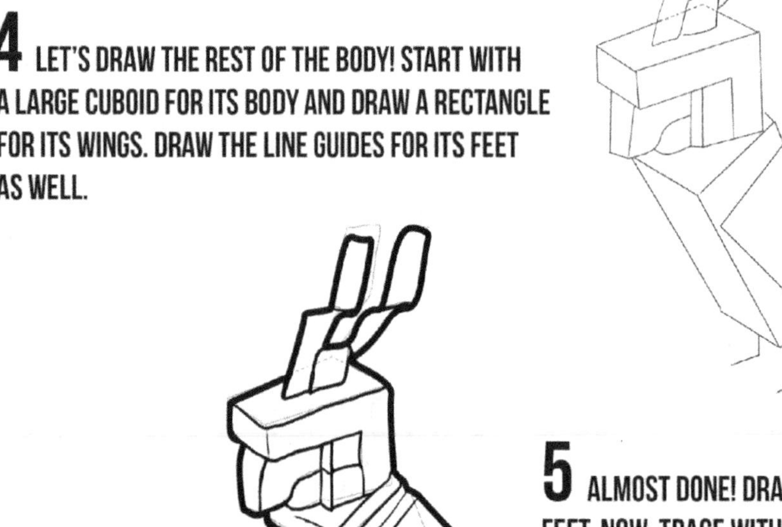

5 ALMOST DONE! DRAW ITS LEG AND FEET. NOW, TRACE WITH THICKER LINES THE FINAL SHAPE OF THE PARROT.

6 TO FINISH DRAWING THE PARROT, DRAW HIS EYE AND TAIL.

 PIG

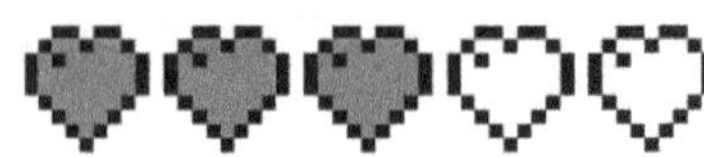

1 START FROM THIS SHAPE TO DRAW PIG'S HEAD.

2 IN THIS STEP, DRAW ITS TORSO

3 NOW, LEGS. START WITH 3 SEPARATE RECTANGLES, CONNECT THEM AND DRAW ONE MORE LIKE IN OUR DRAWING.

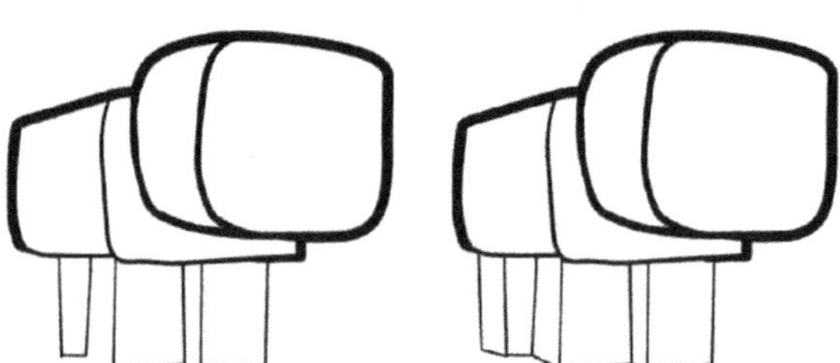

4 TO FINISH YOUR LITTLE PIG, DRAW IT A CUTE FACE, EAR AND A TINY TAIL. YOUR PIG IS CUTE AND DONE!

RABBIT

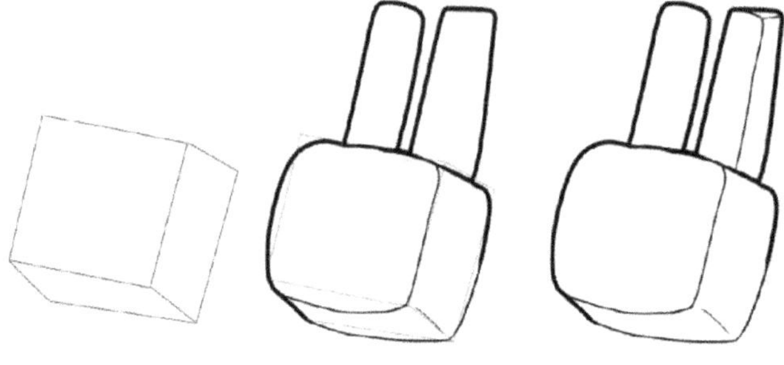

1 FOLLOW THESE THREE EASY STEPS TO FORM THIS RABBIT'S HEAD.

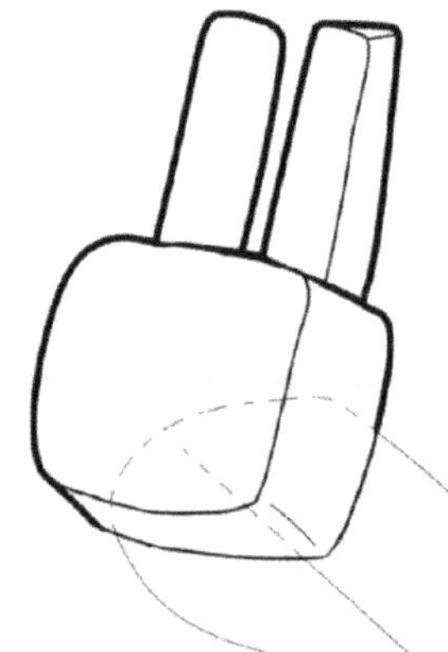

2 NEXT DRAW THE RABBIT'S BODY BY OLLOWING THE SHAPE SHOWN IN THIS IMAGE. ERASE DOTTED LINES.

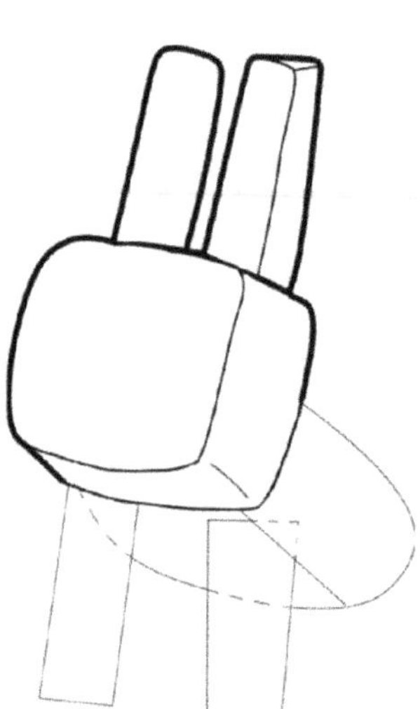

3 NOW, DRAW THE OUTLINE OF HIS LEGS BY DRAWING TWO RECTANGLES.

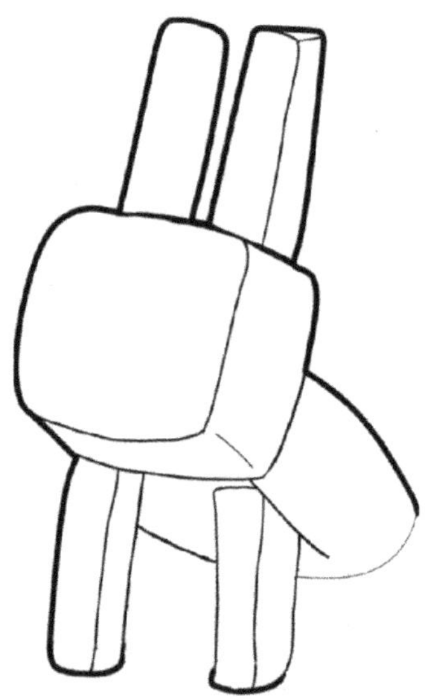

4 DRAW THE SIDES OF THE LEGS TO ADD DIMENSION TO THE DRAWING.

RABBIT

5 TO DRAW HIS BACK LEGS, START BY DRAWING HIS FEET FIRST AS SHOWN IN THE DRAWING.

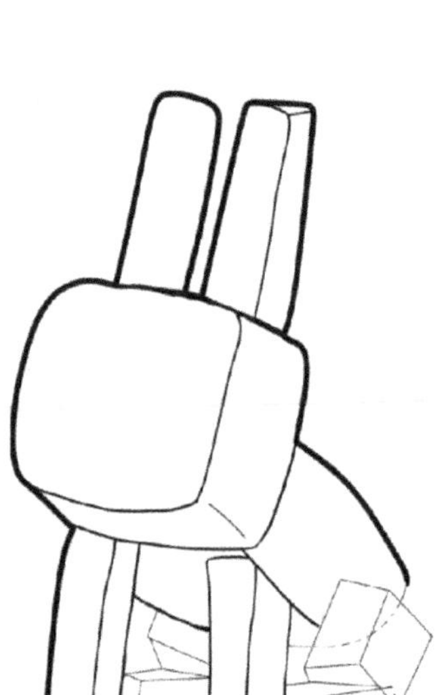

6 NOW CONNECT THE BACK LEG TO ITS FEET. ERASE DOTTED LINES.

7 NOW THAT WE HAVE THE FINAL SHAPE, USE THICKER LINES TO TRACE THE RABBIT'S FULL BODY SHAPE. TO FINISH IT, DRAW HIM A FLUFFY LITTLE TAIL AND CUTE FACE. DON'T FORGET TO DRAW HIS EARS! AFTER YOU ADD SHADINGS AND OTHER DETAILS, IT IS DONE!

POLAR BEAR

DIFFICULTY LEVEL

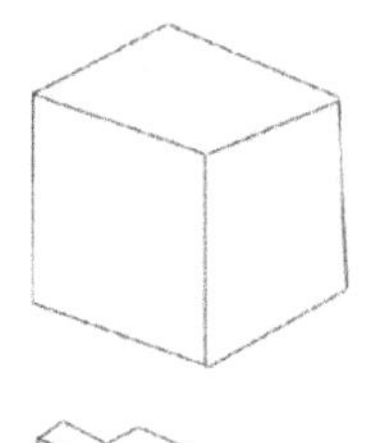 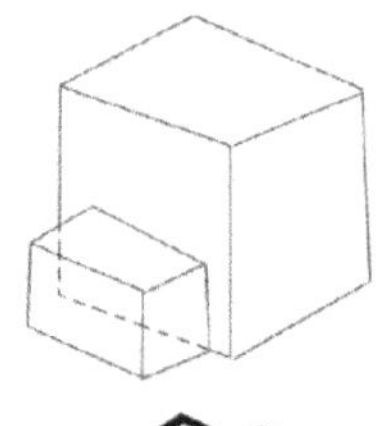

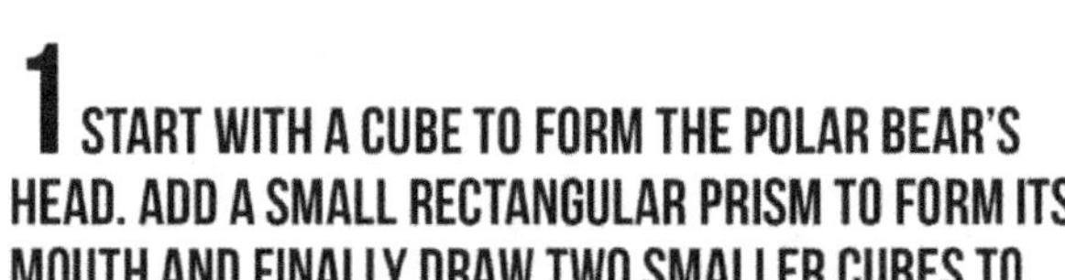

1 START WITH A CUBE TO FORM THE POLAR BEAR'S HEAD. ADD A SMALL RECTANGULAR PRISM TO FORM ITS MOUTH AND FINALLY DRAW TWO SMALLER CUBES TO FORM ITS EARS. TRACE THE HEAD WITH THICKER LINES.

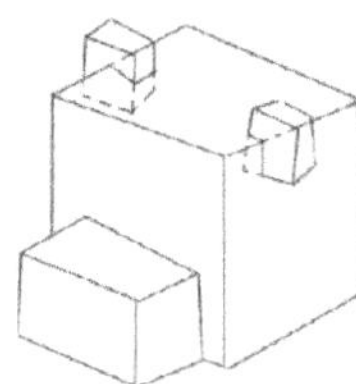 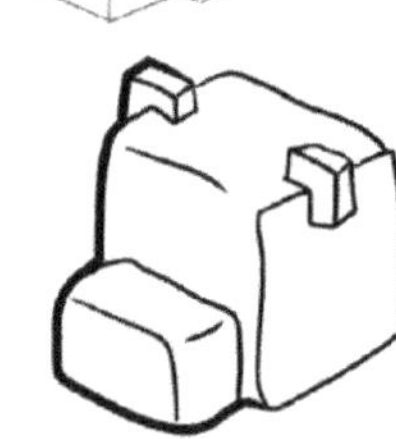

2 TO DRAW THE TORSO, ADD A BIG CUBOID BEHIND THE BEAR'S HEAD JUST LIKE WHAT IS SHOWN IN THE DRAWING.

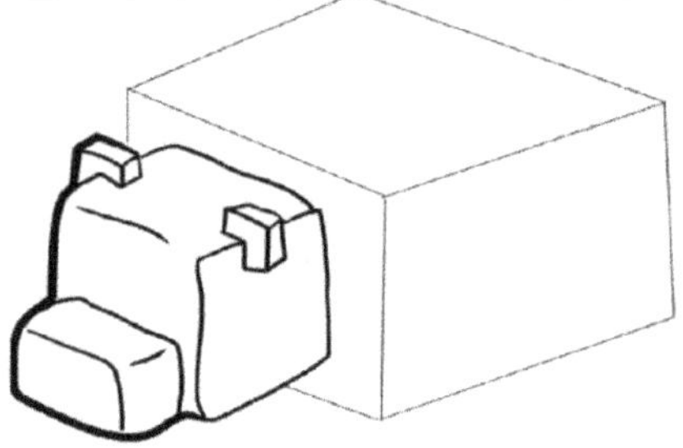

3 NOW UNTO THE SECOND PART OF THE TORSO, DRAW A BIGGER SHAPED CUBE BEHIND THE FIRST PART OF THE TORSO.USING ONE OF THE EDGES AS BASELINE.

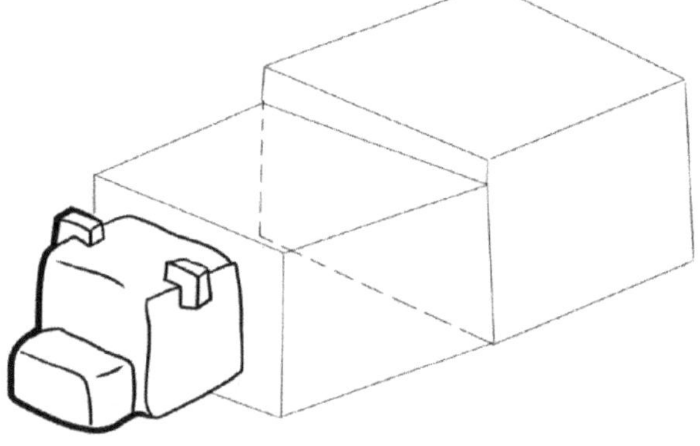

POLAR BEAR

DIFFICULTY LEVEL

4 SHAPE HIS LEGS USING OUR DRAWINGS BELOW:

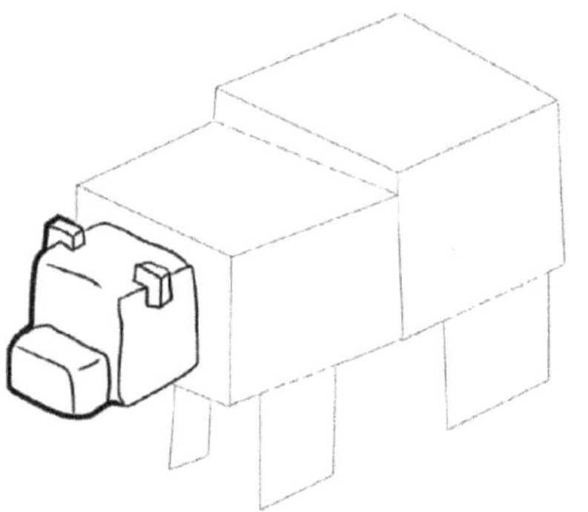

5 NOW WHEN YOU HAVE YOUR FINAL GUIDE, USE THICKER LINES TO DRAW THIS POLAR BEAR FULL BODY.

6 TO FINISH THIS BEAR, DRAW IT A FACE AND CLAWS. SHADING AND SOME DETAILS ON ITS FUR WILL MAKE IT NICE AND PRETTY.

PUFFER FISH

1 START WITH A SQUARE WITH A CIRCLE ON ITS EDGE, AFTER THAT, ADD ONE SMALLER SQUARE ON THE UPPER CROSSING, AND ONE MORE ON THE EDGE OF CIRCLE LINE INSIDE THE SQUARE. DRAW THE SHAPE SHOWN IN THE THIRD DRAWING.

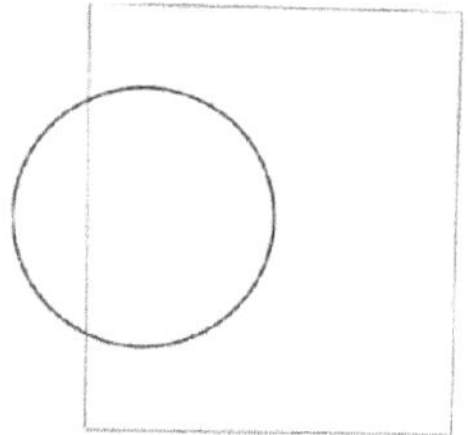 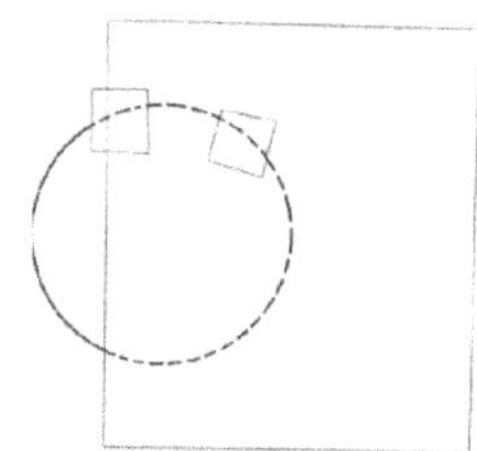 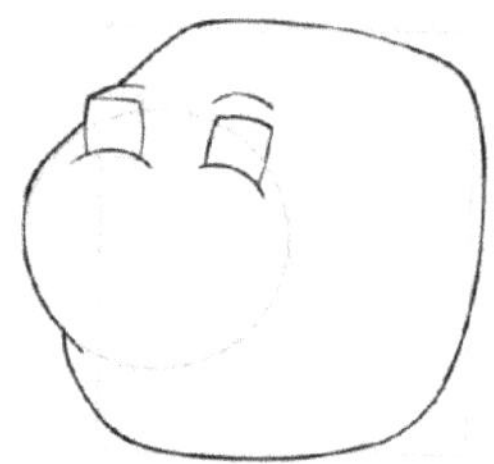

2 ERASE GUIDELINES AND DRAW YOUR FISH FINS AND TAIL.. USE THICKER LINES TO DRAW FINAL SHAPE OF THIS CUTE FISH.

3 TO FINISH PUFFER FISH ADD HER A LOT OF SPIKES. DRAW HER A FACE AND SMALL DETAILS, AND IT IS DONE!

1 START WITH THE SHAPE OF THE SAPLING.
FIRST DRAW THE MAIN TRUNK AND DRAW FEW BRANCHES ON IT.

2 ADD LEAVES ON ITS BRANCHES.

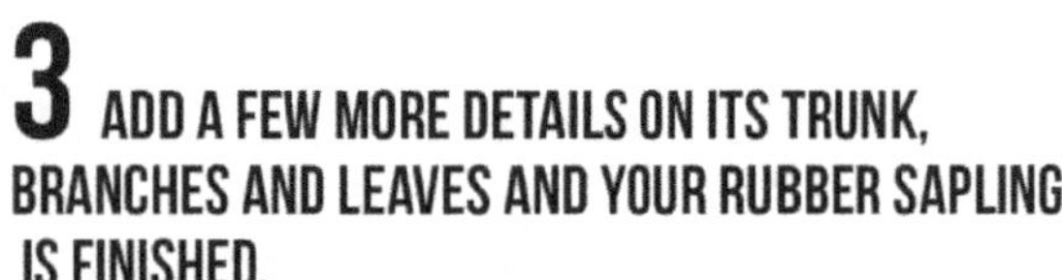

3 ADD A FEW MORE DETAILS ON ITS TRUNK,
BRANCHES AND LEAVES AND YOUR RUBBER SAPLING
IS FINISHED.

SQUID

DIFFICULTY LEVEL

1 OK, THIS ONE IS EASY, SO LET'S BEGIN. START WITH THESE TWO STEPS. FIRST, DRAW THE SQUID'S HEAD AND TWO OF HER TENTACLES.

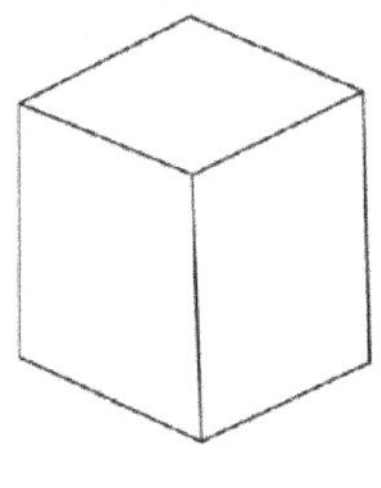
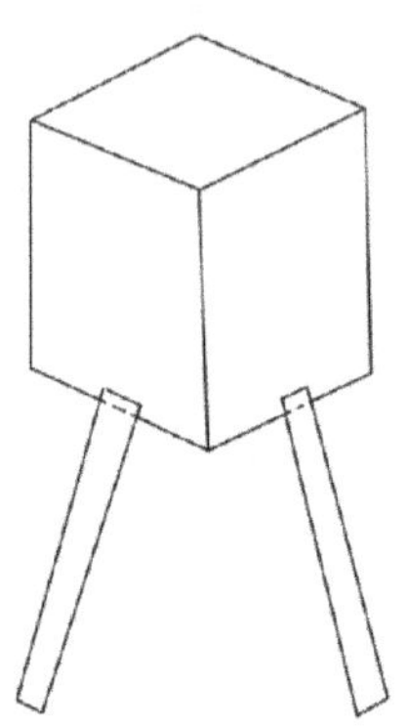

2 AFTER THAT, ADD SOME SIDES TO ITS TENTACLES TO ADD DIMENSION. DRAW 3 MORE TENTACLES.

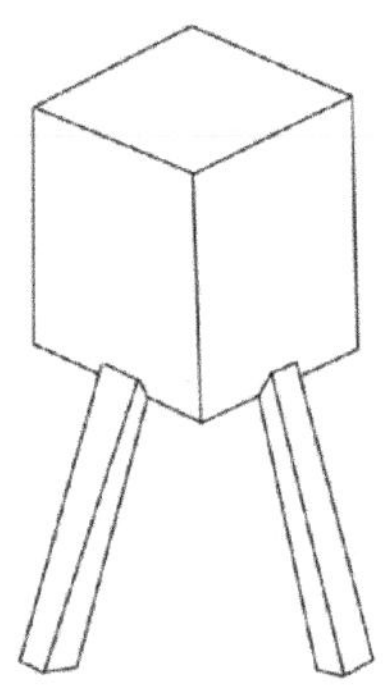
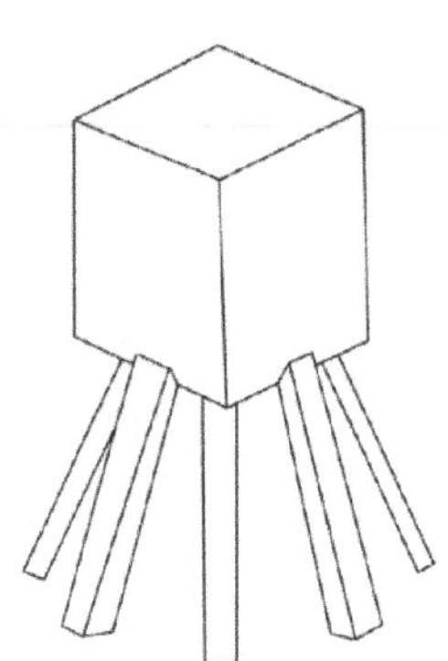
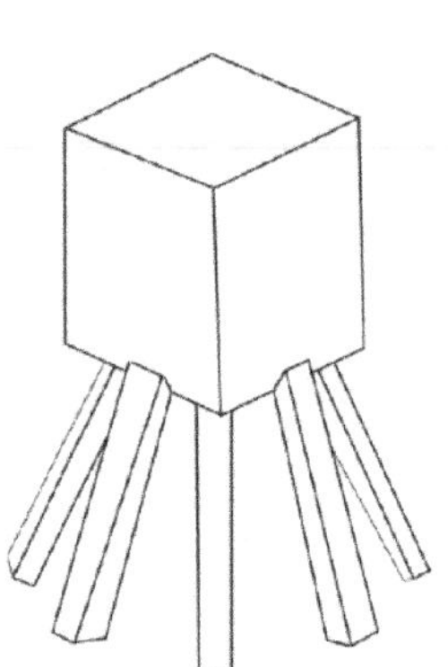

3 ALMOST DONE! USE THICKER LINES TO DRAW THE FINAL SHAPE OF THE SQUID .NOW ADD THE SQUID'S EYES AND DETAILS ON ITS BODY.

SHULKER

1 1. START WITH SHAPING HIS UPPER PART AND FOLLOWING THESE STEPS.

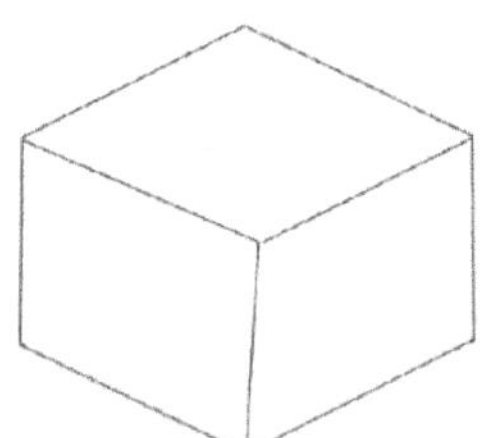 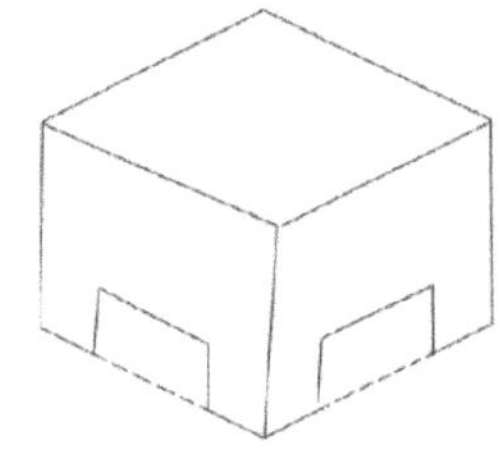 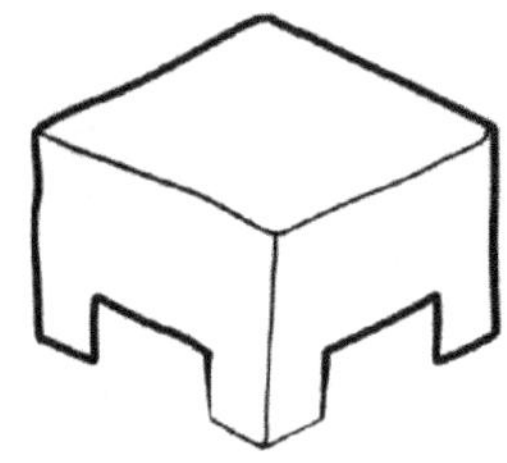

2 NOW FOR THE LOWER PART, FOLLOW THE ILLUSTRATIONS BELOW. IT IS NOT THAT HARD.

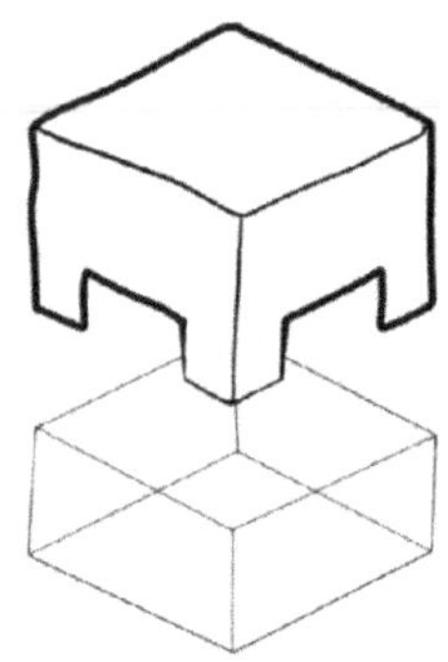 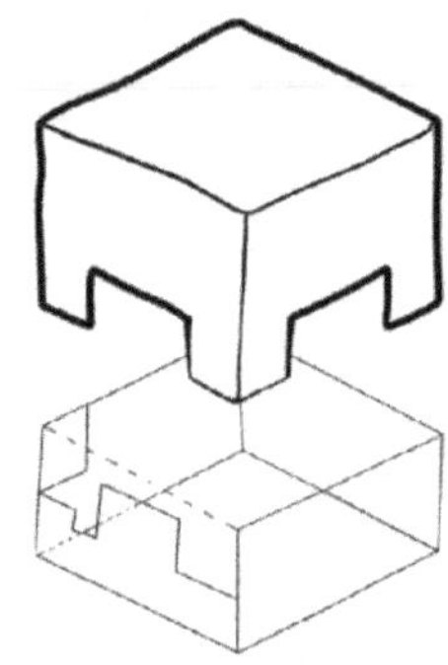 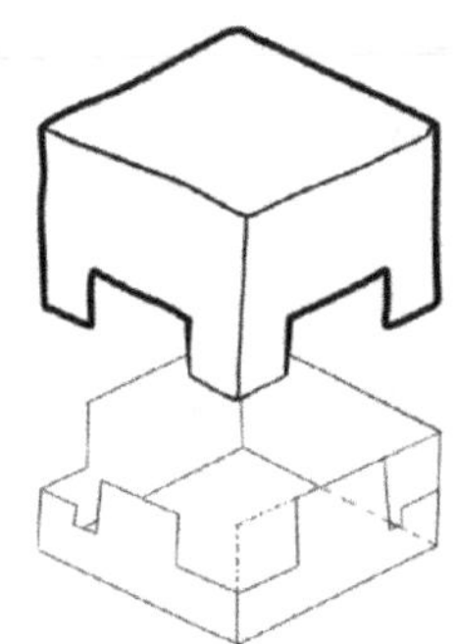 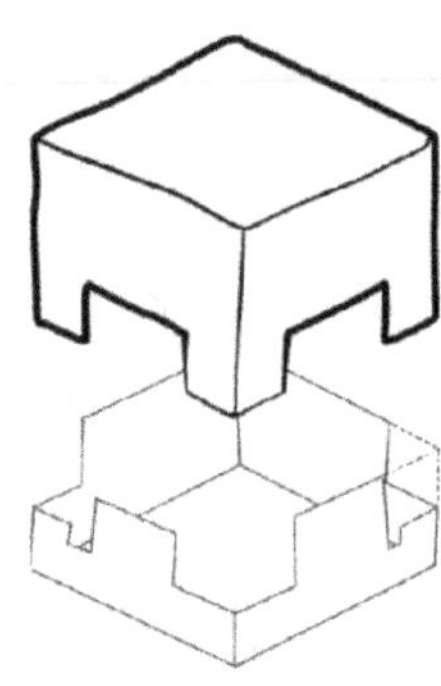

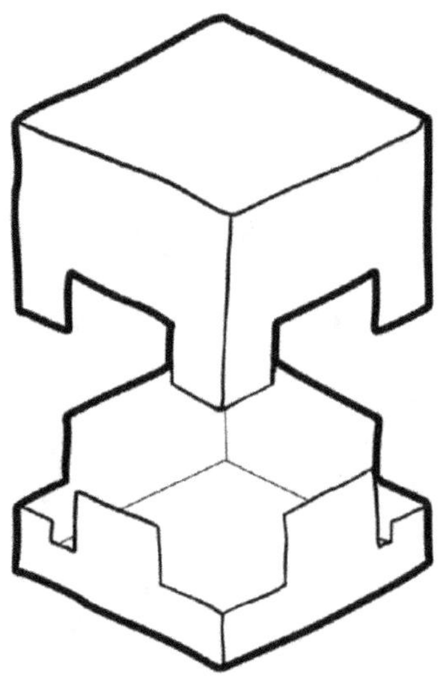

3 USE THICKER LINES TO FORM THE FINAL SHAPE OF HIS SHELL. THIS IS HOW IT SHOULD LOOK LIKE.

SHULKER

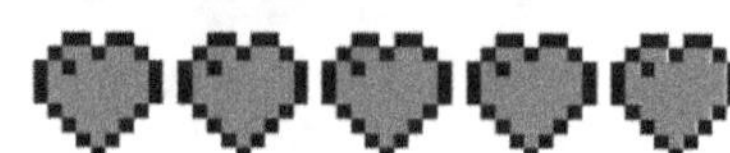

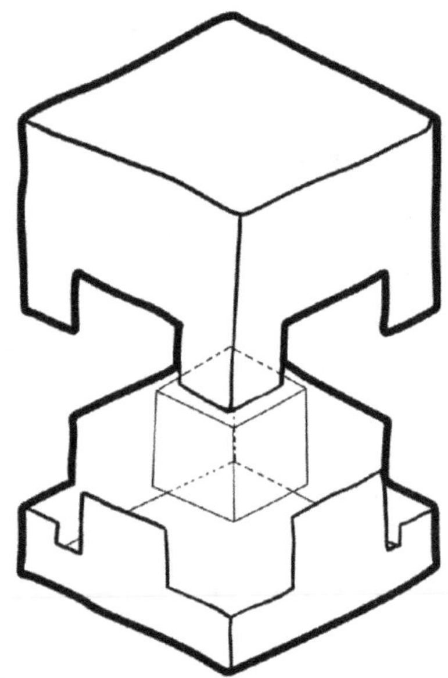

4 NOW FORM HIS MIDDLE PART. REFER TO THE IMAGE TO THE LEFT TO SEE HOW IT IS DONE.

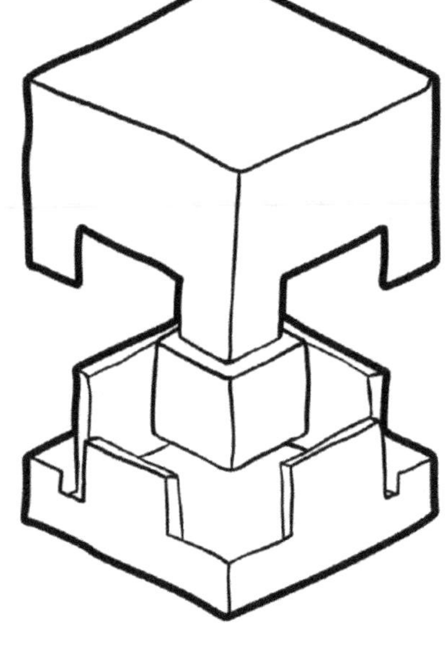

5 ALMOST DONE! USE THICKER LINES TO TRACE THE FINAL SHAPE OF THE SHULKER.

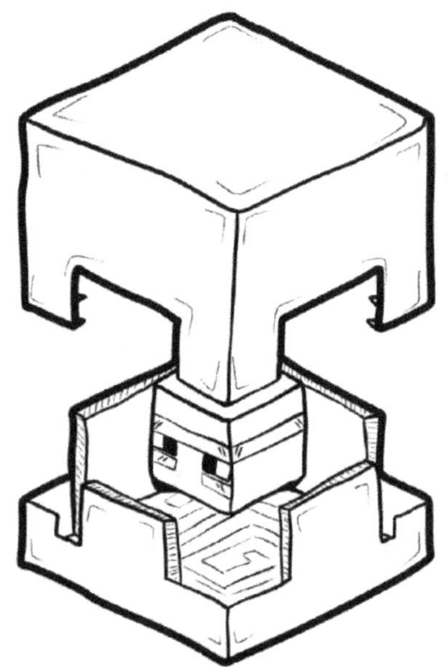

6 NOW WHEN WE HAVE HIS FINAL SHAPE, DRAW HIS FACE AND ADD SMALL DETAILS ON HIS SHELL.

SPRUCE SAPLING

DIFFICULTY LEVEL

1 OH, THIS ONE IS REALLY EASY. MAKE A SHAPE OF A TRUNK. IT SHOULD BE LONG AND POINTY.

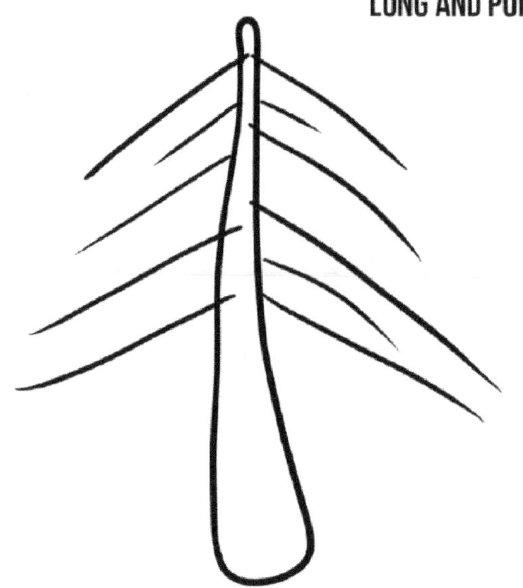

2 NOW, LET'S DRAW SOME LITTLE TWIGS ON IT. JUST DRAW FEW LINES STARTING FROM THE TRUNK.

3 LET'S FINISH IT! DRAW AS MANY LEAVES YOU CAN ON EACH TWIG. TO FINISH IT, ADD SOME SMALL DETAILS ON THE TRUNK AND ON ITS ROOTS.

SKELETON

1 1.LET'S DRAW THIS! START WITH HIS HEAD AND IT SHOULD LOOK LIKE THIS:

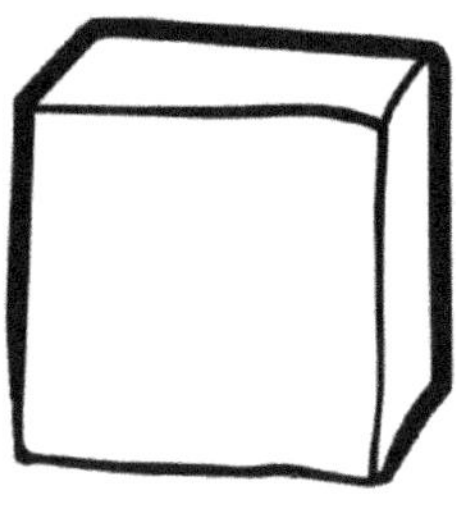

2 NOW DRAW HIS TORSO, A SMALLER CUBE BELOW HIS HEAD.

3 LET'S PROCEED WITH HIS ARM. AFTER DRAWING HIS ARM, FOLLOW THE ILLUSTRATION BELOW AND MAKE HIS TORSO BONY.

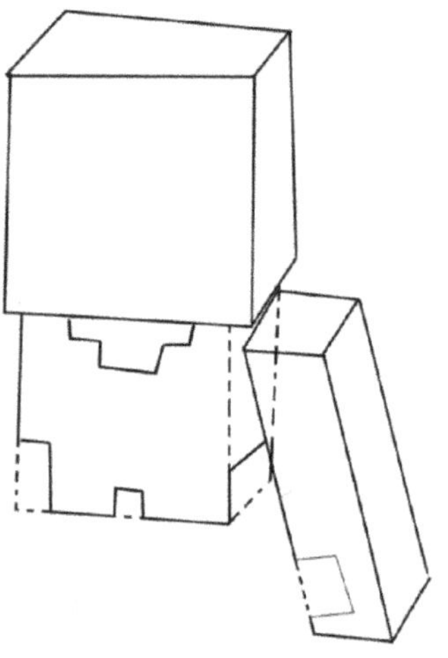

4 WHEN YOU ERASE ALL THE GUIDELINES, THIS IS HOW HIS TORSO SHOULD LOOK LIKE.

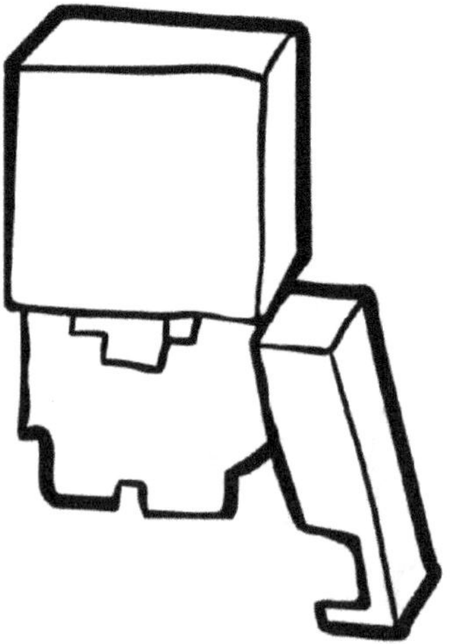

SKELETON

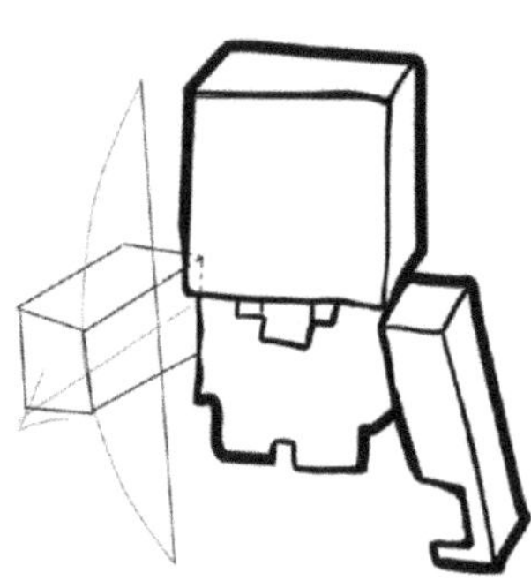

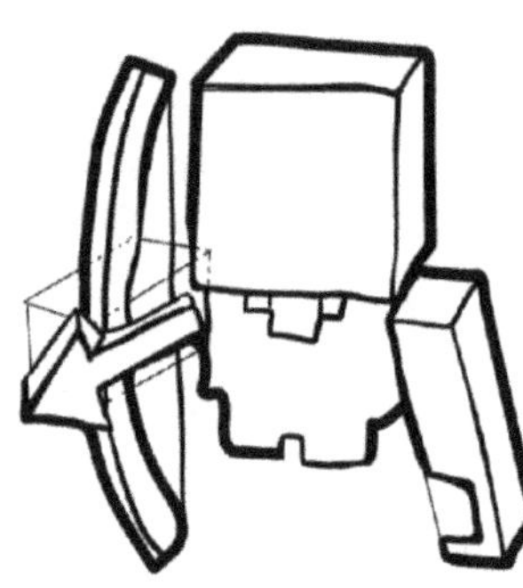

5 STEP BY STEP, LET'S FORM HIS OTHER HAND HOLDING A BOW AND ARROW. START WITH A SKETCH AND AFTER THAT, DRAW THE FINAL SHAPE OF HIS BOW AND ARROW.

6 USE THICKER LINES TO FORM HIS HAND, AND THEN DRAW HIS LOWER BODY JUST LIKE IN OUR DRAWING.

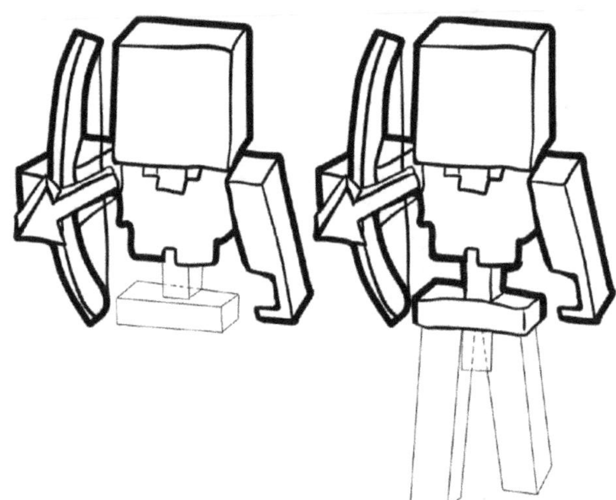

7 TO FINISH SKELETON, USE THICKER LINES TO DRAW HIS LEGS. DRAW HIM A FACE AND MORE HOLES IN HIS TORSO. SOME SHADING AND SMALL DETAILS ON HIM WILL MAKE HIM GREAT!

SNOW GOLEM

1 FOLLOW THESE EASY STEPS TO START
SHAPING SNOW GOLEM'S HEAD AND UPPER BODY!

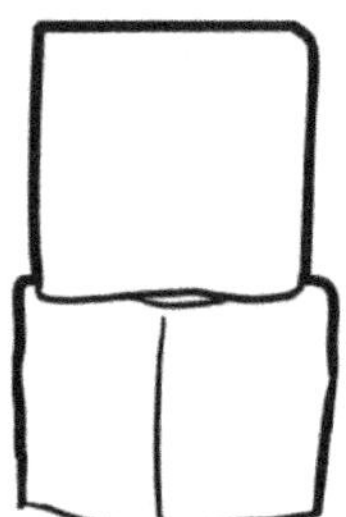

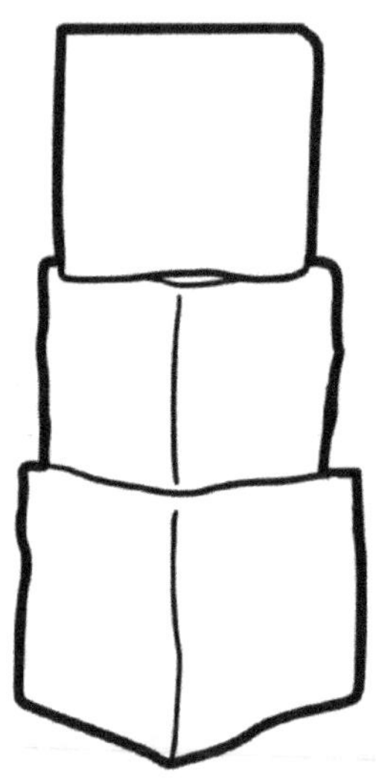

2 NOW, DRAW HIS FULL BODY JUST
LIKE THE DRAWING ON THE LEFT

3 DRAW THIN LINES FOR HIS ARMS AND
REMOVE LINE GUIDES.

4 TO FINISH YOUR SNOW GOLEM, DRAW HIM
A FACE AND SOME DETAILS ON HIS BODY.
DOESN'T HE LOOK COOL?

SPIDER

DIFFICULTY LEVEL

1 1. TO DRAW A SPIDER, START BY DRAWING A CUBE.

2 NOW, LET'S SHAPE THE OTHER PART OF HIS BODY. IT IS JUST A LARGER CUBE BEHIND THE FIRST ONE.

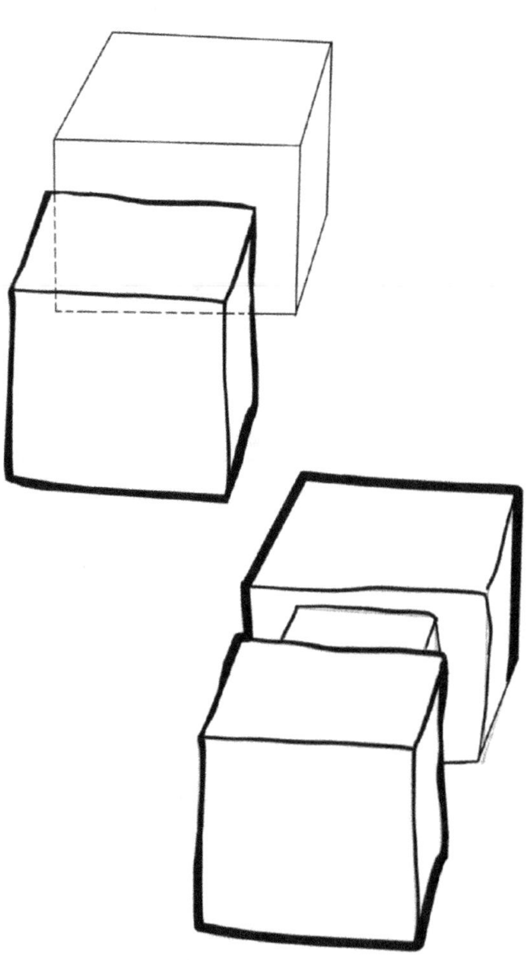

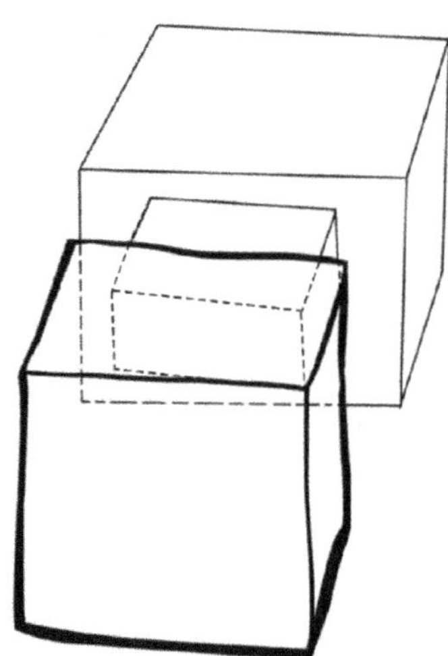

3 THEN, FOLLOW THE DRAWING ABOVE WHICH SHOWS A PART THAT CONNECTS THE TWO CUBES.

4 WHEN WE ERASE ALL GUIDELINES, THIS IS HOW HIS BODY SHOULD LOOK LIKE.

SPIDER

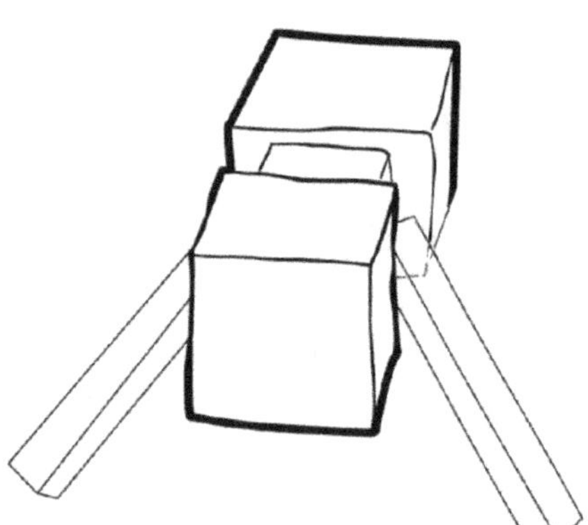

5 LET'S START SHAPING HIS LEGS! START WITH TWO ON THE OPPOSITE SIDES OF HIS BODY. MAKE IT LOOK LIKE IT IS STARTING FROM THE MIDDLE PART OF HIS BODY.

6 NOW, LET'S SHAPE ALL OF HIS LEGS JUST LIKE IN OUR DRAWING.

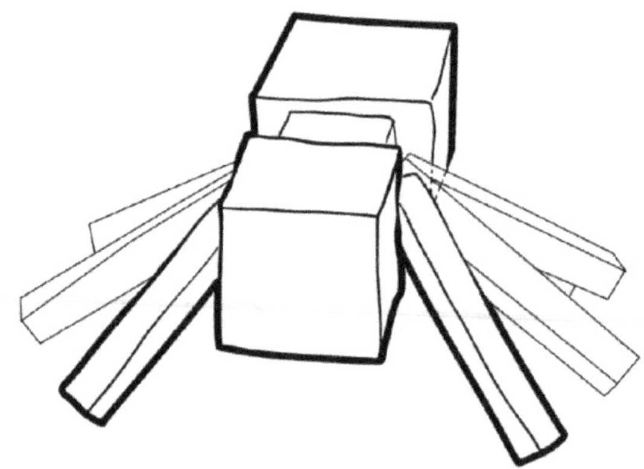

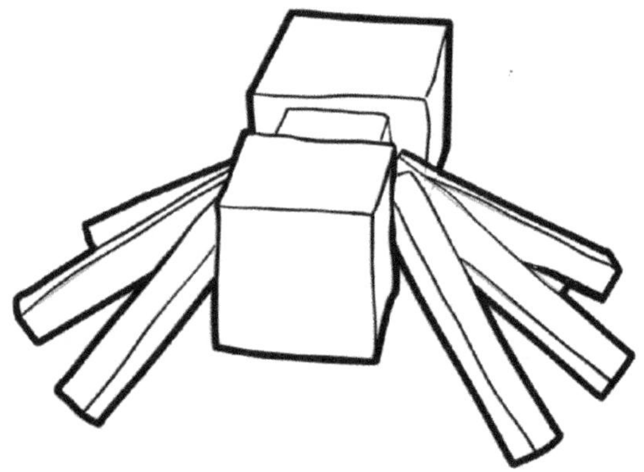

7 USE GUIDELINES TO DRAW HIS FINAL SHAPE WITH THICKER LINES.

8 TO FINISH DRAWING THE SPIDER, DRAW HIS FACE. ADD SHADINGS AND SOME SPOTS ON HIS BODY TO MAKE HIM LOOK REALLY COOL.

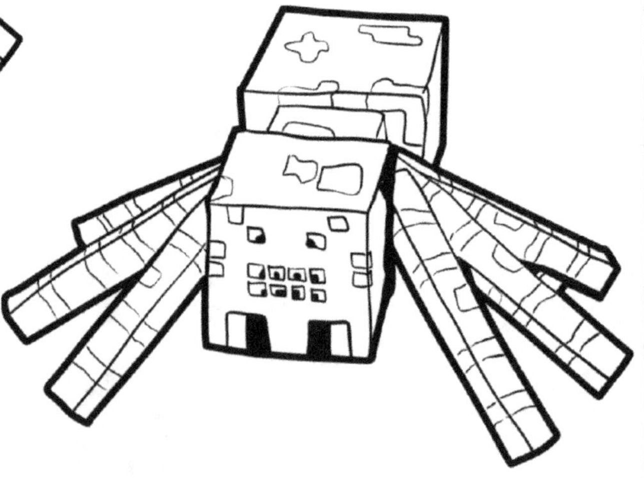

1 START WITH THE SHAPE OF HIS HEAD.

2 THEN DRAW HIS TORSO.

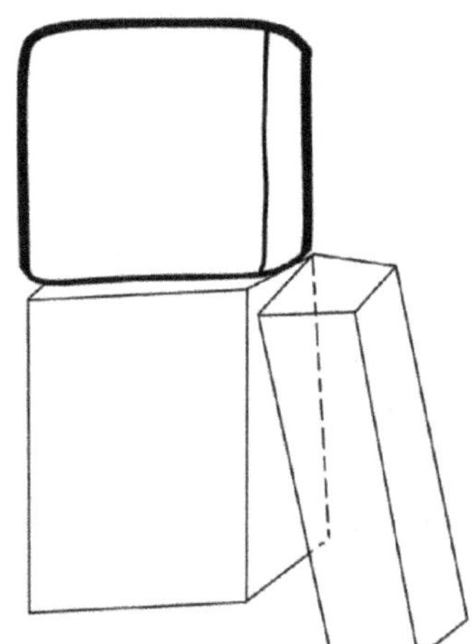

3 NOW LET'S SHAPE HIS LEFT ARM.
FOLLOW THE DRAWING AND ERASE DOTTED LINES.

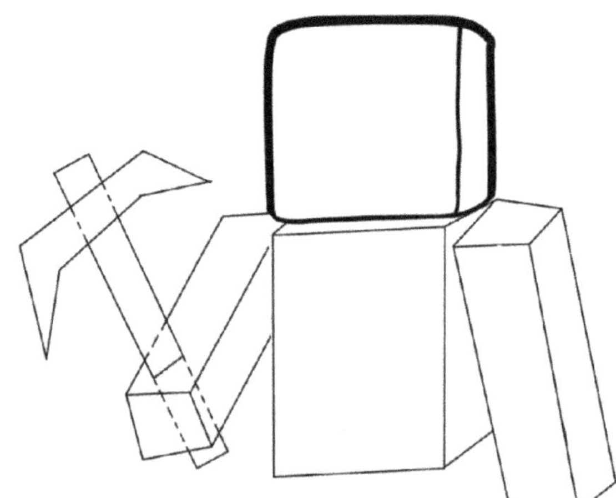

4 LET'S DRAW HIS OTHER ARM. FIRST DRAW
AN ARM THEN SHAPE A PICKAXE.

STEVE

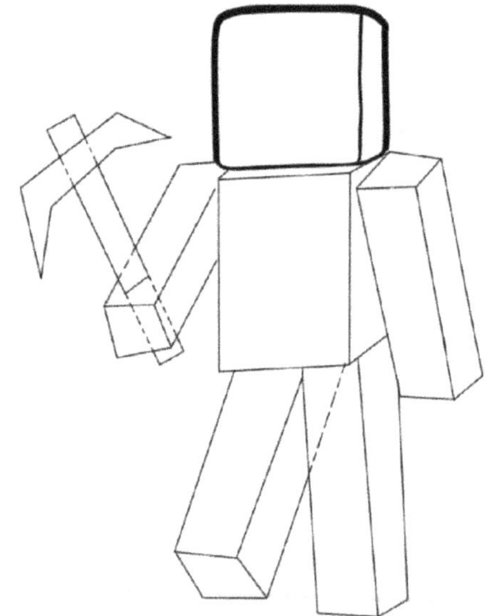

5 NOW THAT WE HAVE THE SHAPE OF HIS UPPER BODY, LET'S DRAW HIS LEGS JUST LIKE IN THE PICTURE.

6 USE THICKER LINES TO OUTLINE THE FINAL SHAPE OF STEVE'S BODY.

7 TO FINISH DRAWING STEVE, DRAW HIS FACE AND HAIR. ADD SOME SHADINGSAND DETAILS ON HIS CLOTHES AND PICKAXE. YOUR STEVE IS DONE.

SWORD

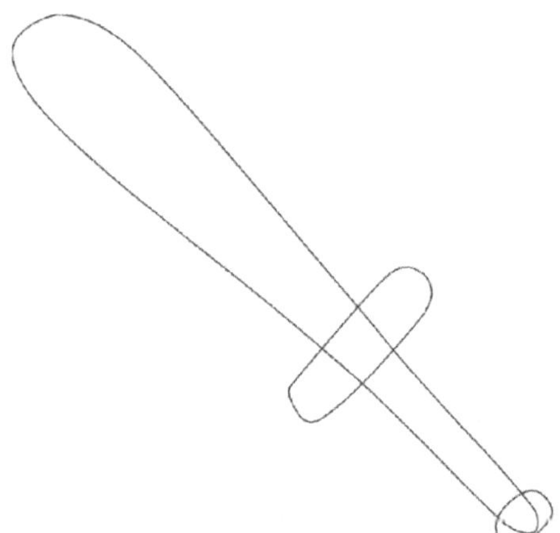

1 SHAPE A SWORD USING THESE THREE SHAPES.

2 NOW, LET'S MAKE IT POINTY! FOLLOW THE DRAWING ABOVE AND FORM A SWORD.

3 ADD LINES ON THE SWORD TO SEPARATE THE HANDLE FROM THE BLADE. ADD DETAILS ON ITS BLADE TO MAKE IT LOOK REALLY SHARP.

4 ALMOST DONE! NOW YOU CAN FINISH YOUR DRAWING WITH SOME SMALL DETAILS ON THE HANDLE.

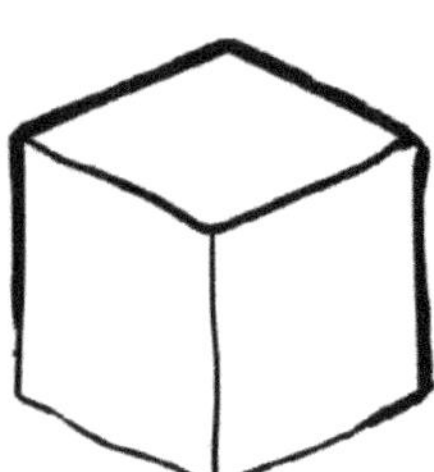

1 OKAY, FIRST STEP IS EASY SO LET'S BEGIN! START WITH A CUBE FOR HIS HEAD.

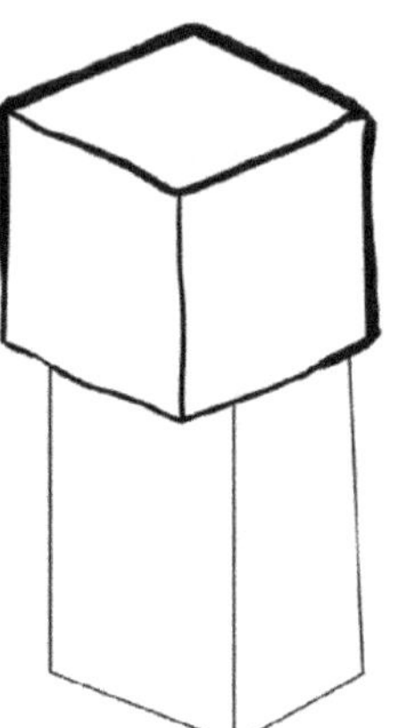

2 NOW, DRAW HIM A TORSO.

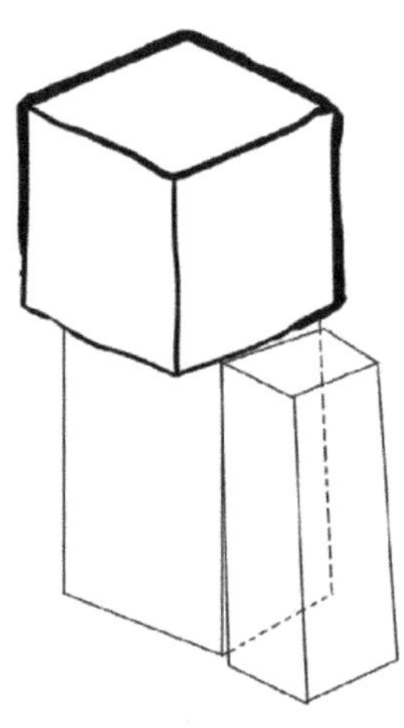

3 NEXT STEP IS HIS LEFT ARM. DRAW SHAPE OF IT NEXT TO THE BODY.

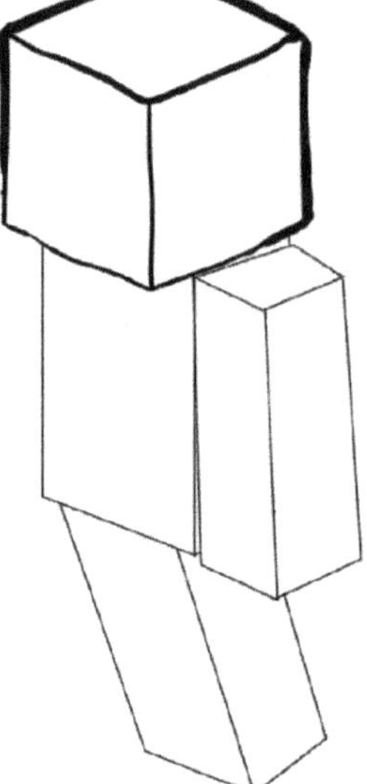

4 WE CAN NOW DRAW HIM HIS LEGS FOLLOWING THE DRAWING ABOVE.

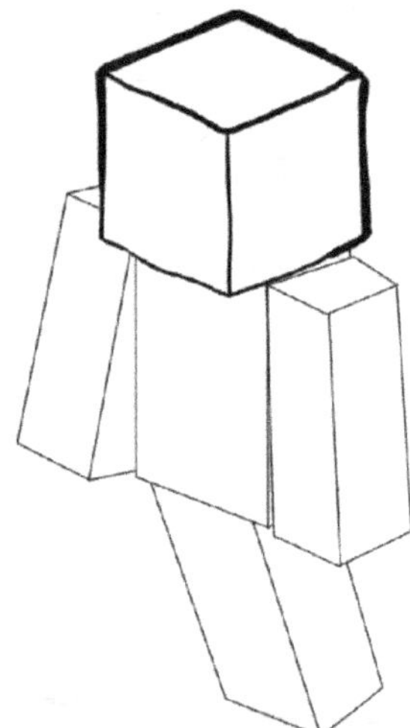

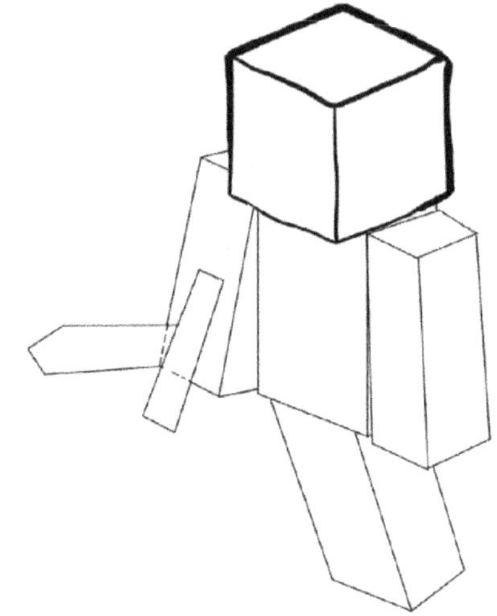

5 NOW DRAW HIM HIS OTHER ARM.

6 LET'S DRAW THE SHAPE OF HIS SWORD IN HIS RIGHT HAND.

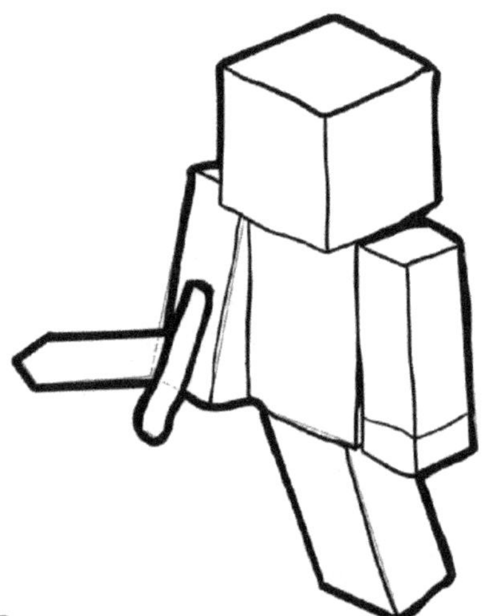

7 USE THICKER LINES TO TRACE THE FINAL SHAPE OF HIS BODY. ERASE ALL GUIDELINES.

8 FINALLY, LET'S DRAW HIS LEFT WING. AFTER THAT, ADD HIS FACE, SOME DETAILS ON HIS SWORD AND HIS BODY.

WOLF

DIFFICULTY LEVEL

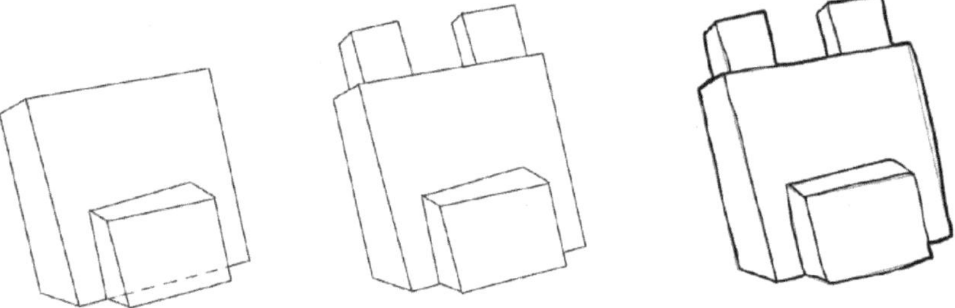

1 FOLLOW THESE THREE EASY STEPS TO FORM THE WOLF'S HEAD. START WITH A BIG CUBE AND THEN DRAW SMALLER CUBES FOR HIS EARS AND MOUTH.

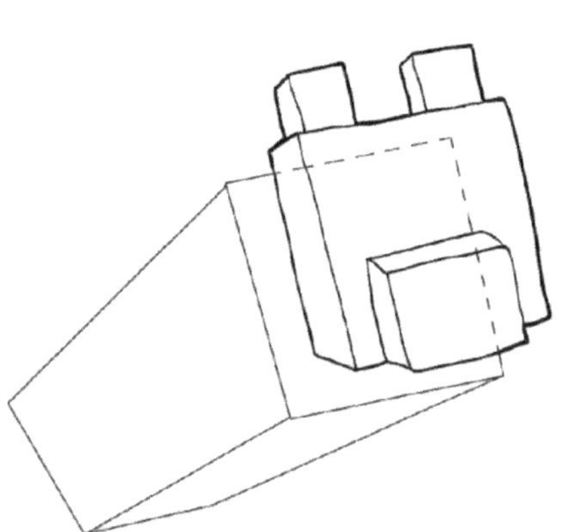

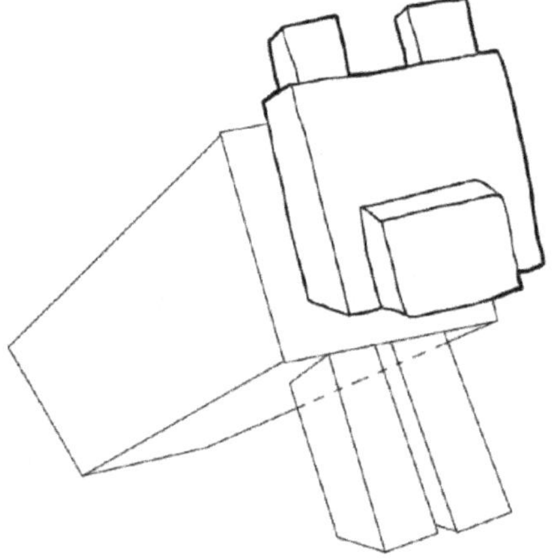

2 FOLLOW THE DRAWING AND ADD HIM A TORSO.

3 TO DRAW HIS FRONT LEGS, FOLLOW THE DRAWING ABOVE.

WOLF

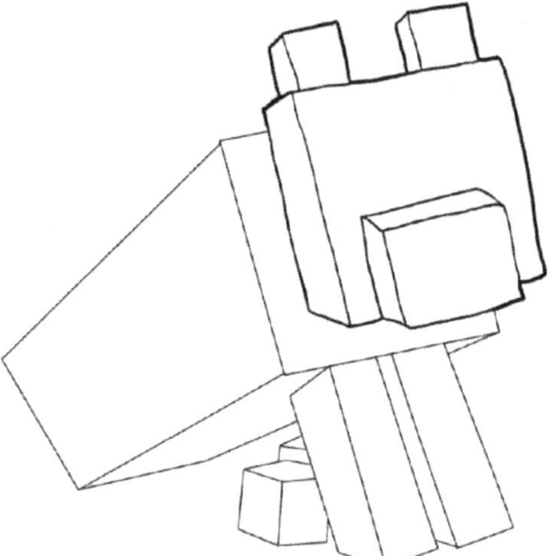

4 TO FORM HIS BACK LEGS, START FROM THE PAWS. SHAPE IT LIKE TWO SMALL CUBES.

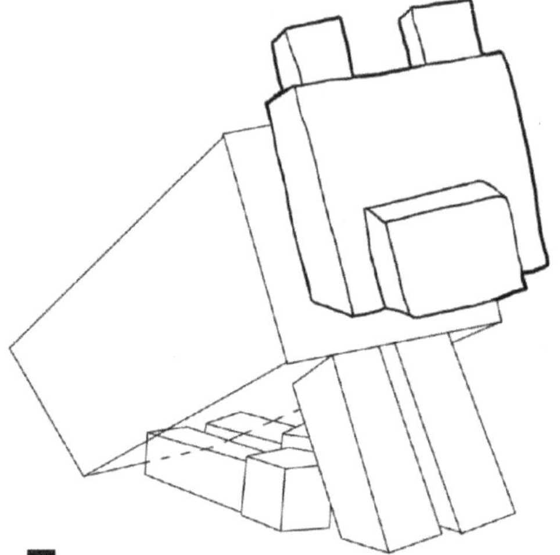

5 NOW DRAW THE UPPER PART OF HIS LEGS. ERASE ALL DOTTED LINES, AND WE HAVE HIS SHAPE!

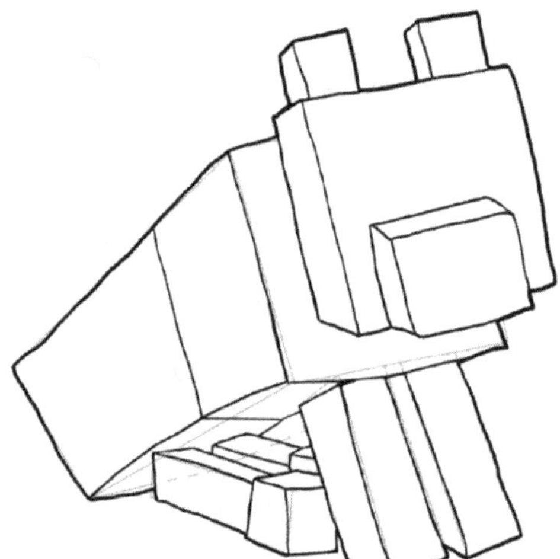

6 USE THICKER LINES TO TRACE THE FINAL SHAPE OF THE WOLF'S BODY. ERASE ALL LINE GUIDES AND THERE HE IS!

7 ALMOST DONE NOW! DRAW HIM A FACE, HIS TAIL, AND FEW SPOTS ON HIS BODY. ISN'T HE CUTE?

ZOMBIE

1 TO START, DRAW A CUBE FOR HIS HEAD.

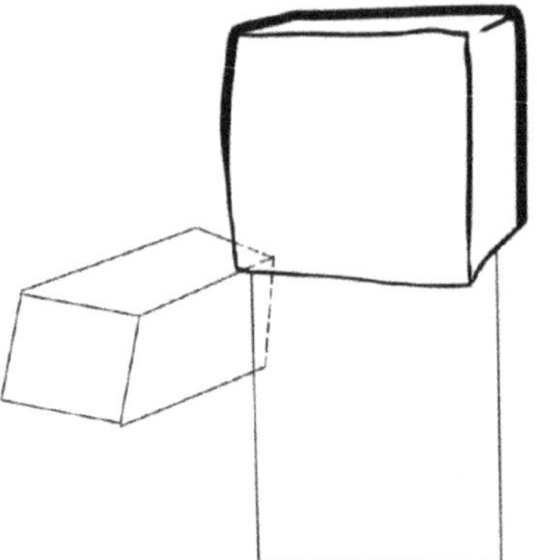

2 DRAW A RECTANGLE FOR HIS TORSO AND SHAPE HIS RIGHT ARM.

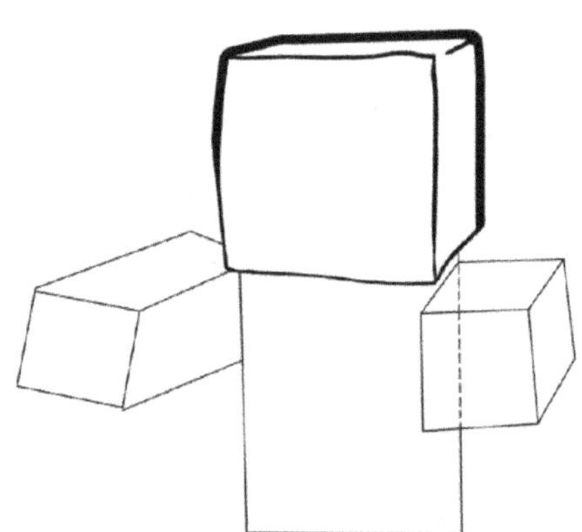

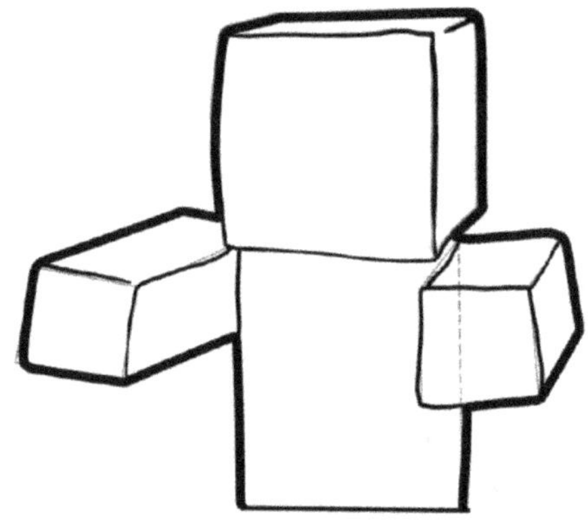

3 NOW, DRAW THE LEFT ARM AND THEN SHAPE HIS UPPER BODY WITH THICKER LINES.

ZOMBIE

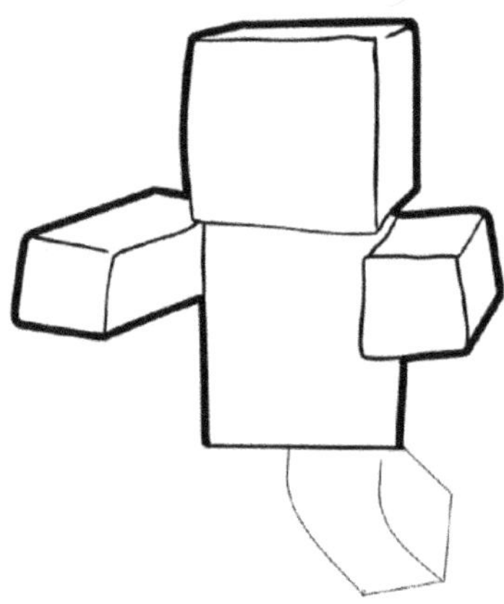

4 DRAW ONE OF HIS LEGS.

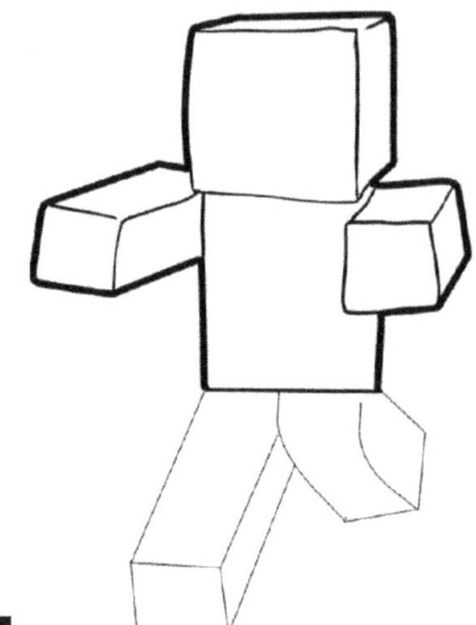

5 NOW YOU CAN SHAPE ANOTHER LEG FOLLOWING OUR DRAWING.

6 NOW WHEN WE HAVE THE SHAPE OF HIS BODY, LET'S FINISH THE DRAWING.

7 TO FINISH DRAWING THE ZOMBIE, MAKE HIS CLOTHES OLD AND DRAW HIS FACE WITH FEW SPOTS ON HIS HEAD.

VINDICATOR

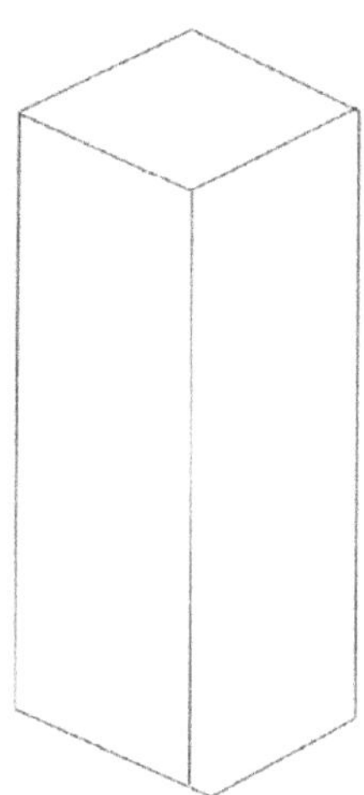

1 START BY DRAWING A VERTICAL RECTANGULAR PRISM. SEPARATE HIS BODY AND HEAD BY ADDING A HORIZONTAL LINE ON THE UPPER PART OF THE PRISM. DRAW HIM HIS NOSE

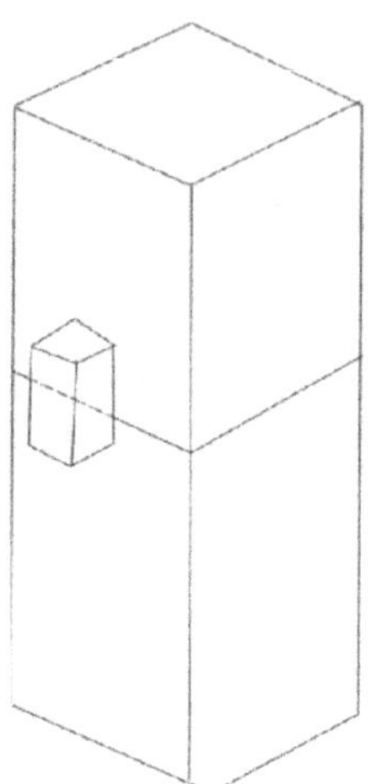

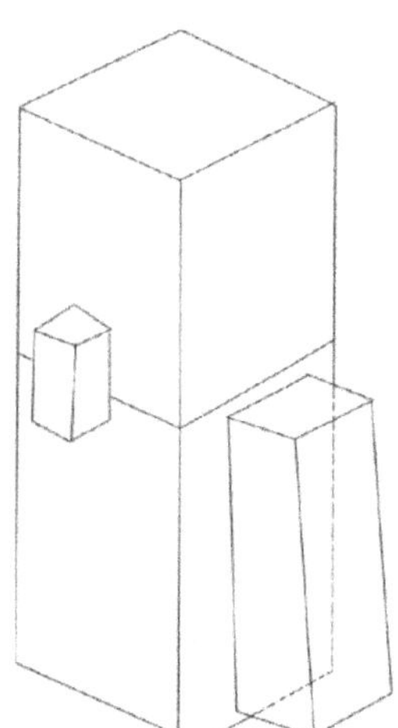

2 DRAW THE SHAPE SHOWN ABOVE WHERE HIS ARM SHOULD BE.

3 FOLLOW THE LINE GUIDES AND DRAW THE FINAL SHAPE OF HIS UPPER BODY IN A SUIT.

VINDICATOR

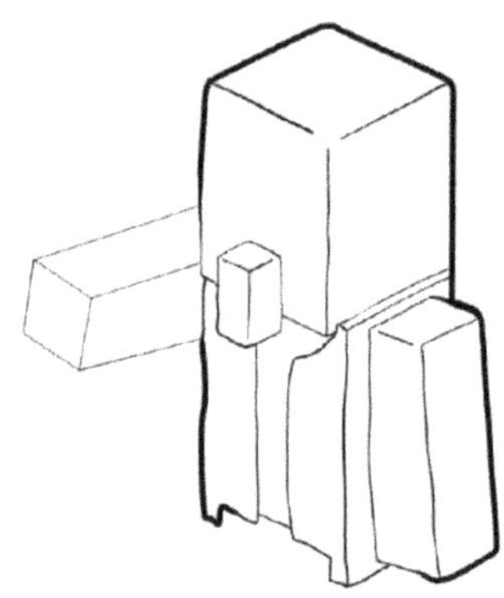

4 NOW, DRAW THE SHAPE OF HIS OTHER ARM.

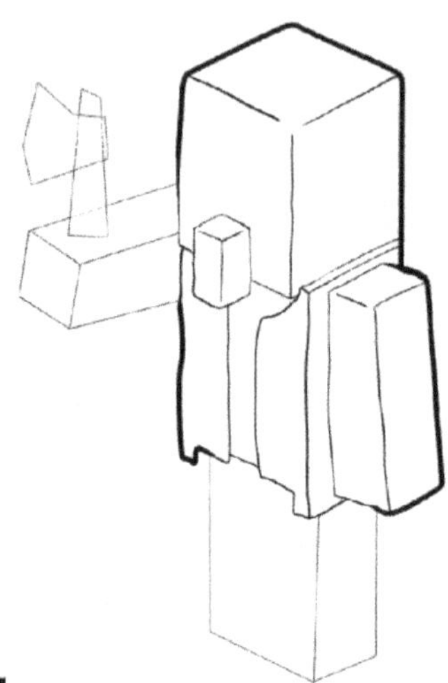

5 NEXT STEP ARE LEGS AND A SHAPE OF AN AXE WHICH HE IS HOLDING.

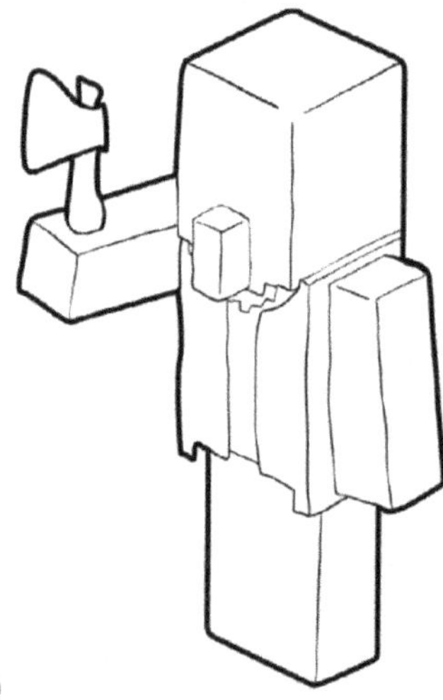

6 USE THICKER LINES TO DRAW THE FINAL SHAPE OF HIS LOWER BODY AND HIS AXE.

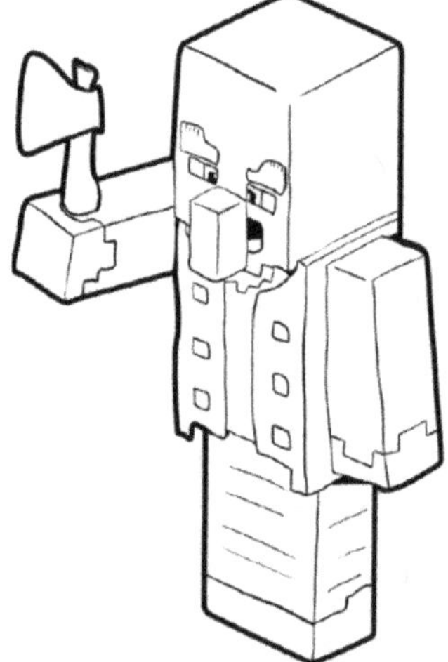

7 TO FINISH THIS DRAWING, DRAW HIS FACE AND ADD DETAILS ON HIS CLOTHES. USE SHADES AND THIN LINES TO MAKE HIM LOOK SCARY.

DIFFICULTY LEVEL

1 LET'S START FROM THE TOP! TO DRAW WITCH HAT YOU SHOULD FOLLOW THESE STEPS:

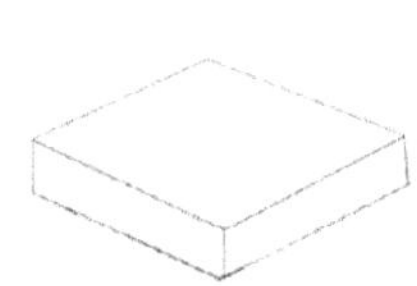 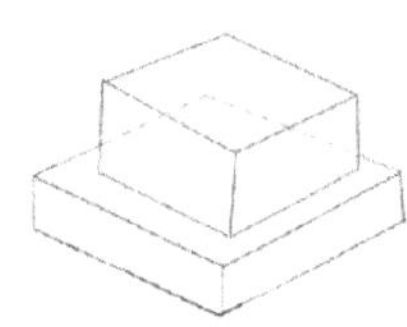 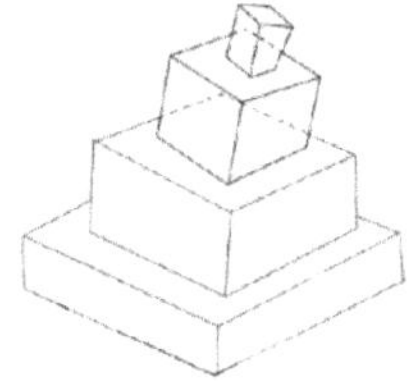 

2 NOW, DRAW A RECTANGULAR PRISM TO FORM HER BODY.

3 SEPARATE HER BODY AND HEAD BY ADDING A HORIZONTAL LINE ON THE UPPER PART OF THE PRISM.

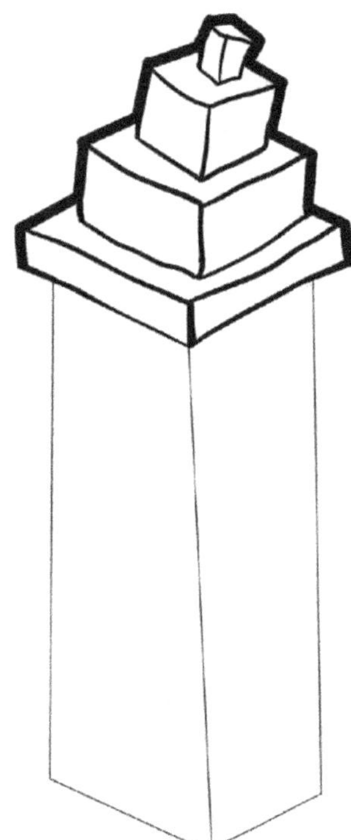

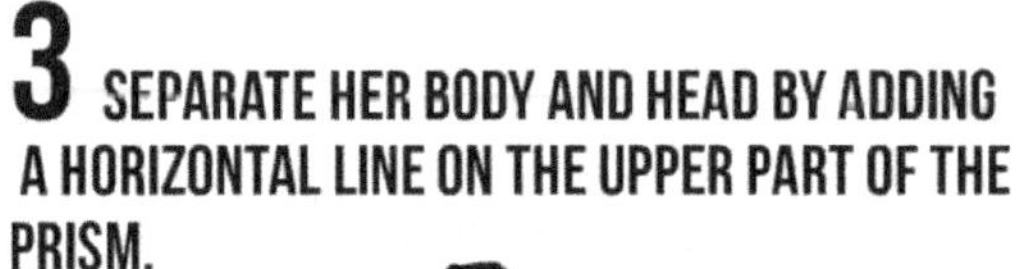

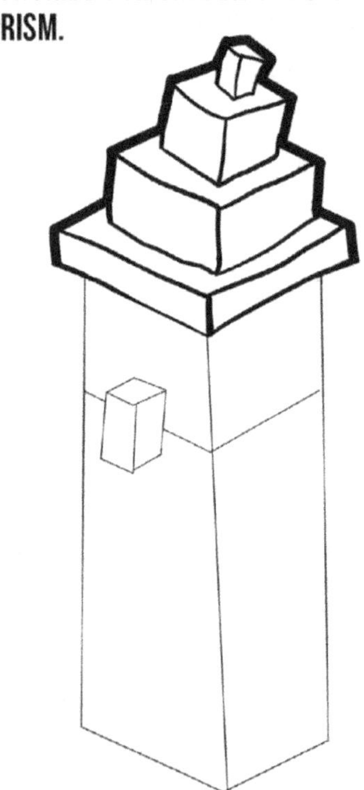

WITCH

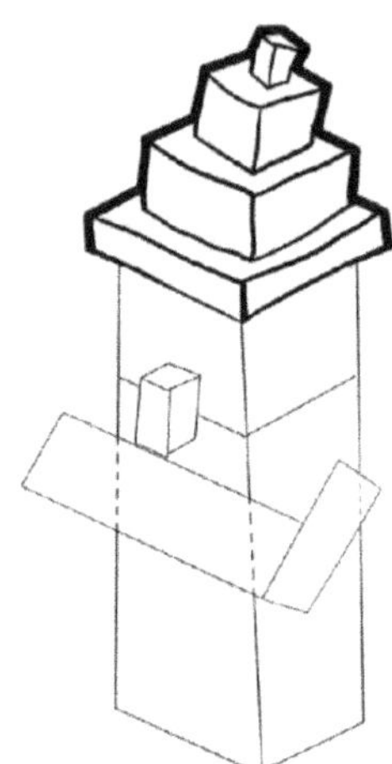

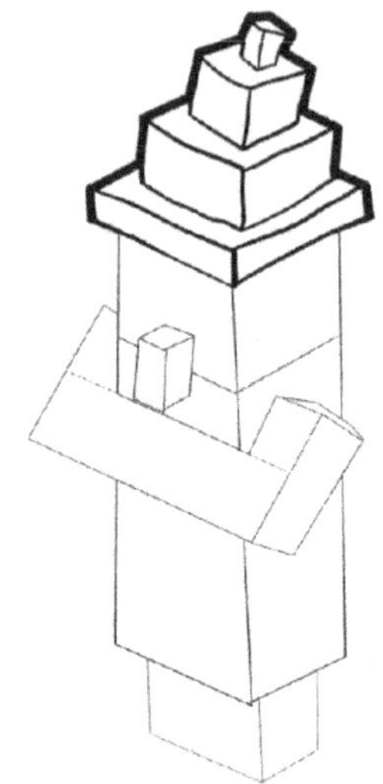

4 TO START FORMING HER HANDS, DRAW A RECTANGLE UNDER HER NOSE. AFTER THAT, DRAW SMALLER ONE, JUST LIKE IN OUR DRAWING.

5 TO FINISH WITCH'S HANDS, FOLLOW OUR DRAWING. ADD HER LEGS. ERASE DOTTED LINES - AND WE HAVE A FULL SHAPE OF HER BODY.

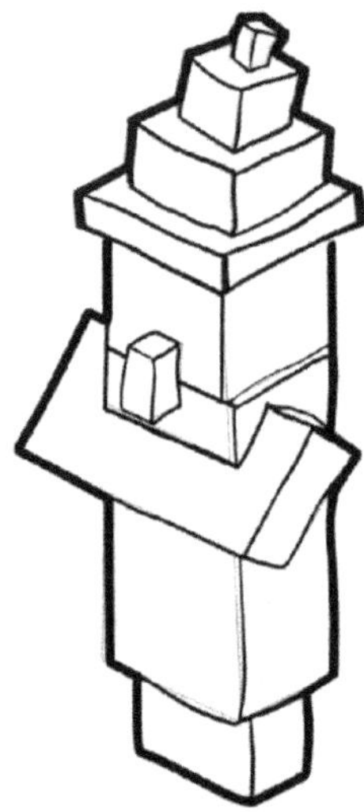

6 NOW, WE HAVE THE SHAPE OF HER BODY. USE THICKER LINES TO DRAW HER FULL SHAPE, JUST LIKE THIS!

7 ALMOST DONE! DRAW HER A FACE, MOLE ON HER NOSE AND SOME DETAILS ON HER HAT AND CLOTHES. NOW SHE IS FINISHED!

WITHER

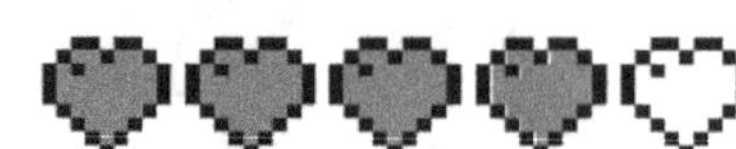

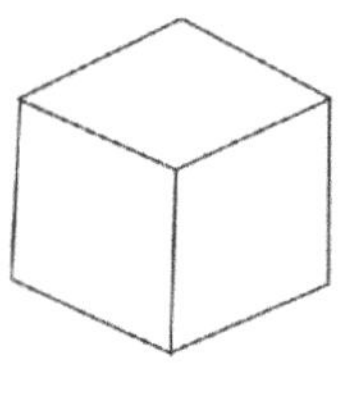
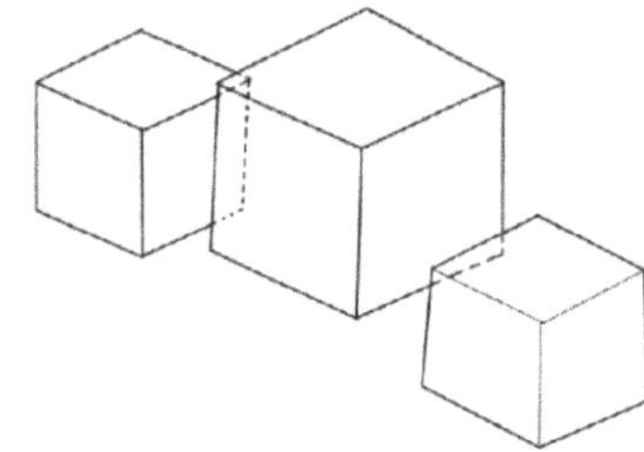
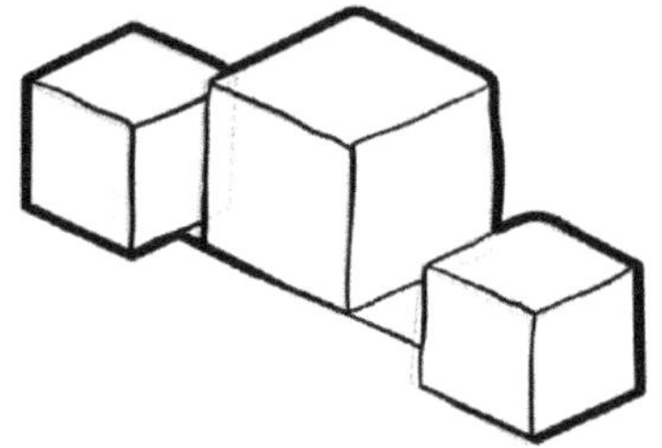

1 FORM HIS THREE HEADS SIMPLY BY DRAWING THREE DIFFERENT CUBES STANDING IN LINE. USE OUR THIRD DRAWING TO CONNECT IT AND MAKE A FINAL FORM.

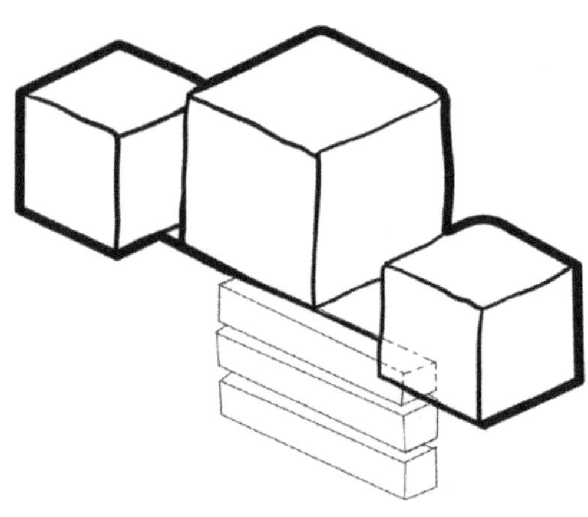

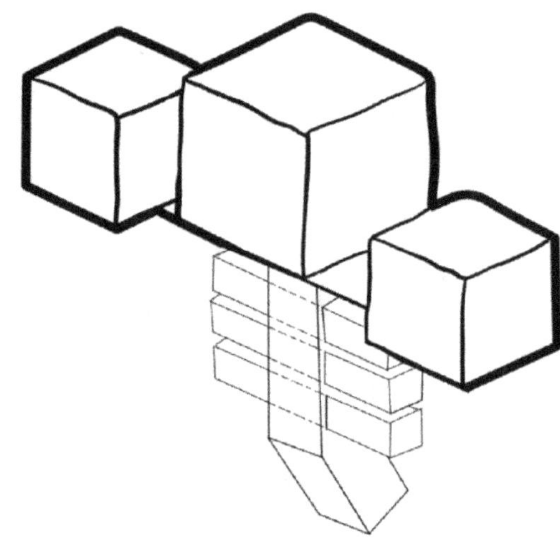

2 FOLLOW THIS STEP AND START FORMING HIS TORSO.

3 WE ARE PROGRESSING! NOW, DRAW A SHAPE WHICH CONNECTS THE SHAPES FROM STEP 2.

WITHER

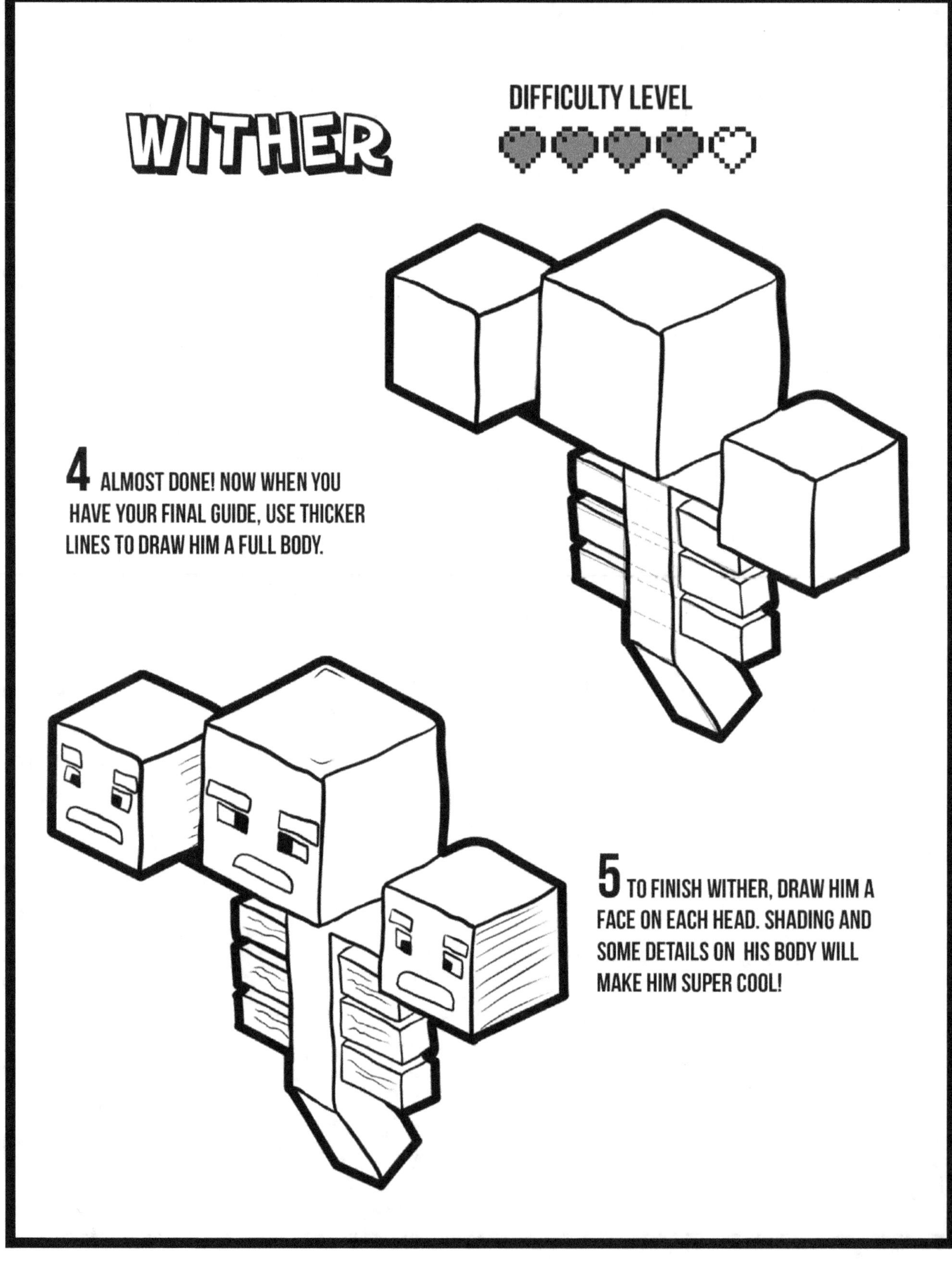

4 ALMOST DONE! NOW WHEN YOU HAVE YOUR FINAL GUIDE, USE THICKER LINES TO DRAW HIM A FULL BODY.

5 TO FINISH WITHER, DRAW HIM A FACE ON EACH HEAD. SHADING AND SOME DETAILS ON HIS BODY WILL MAKE HIM SUPER COOL!

ZOMBIE PIGMAN

DIFFICULTY LEVEL

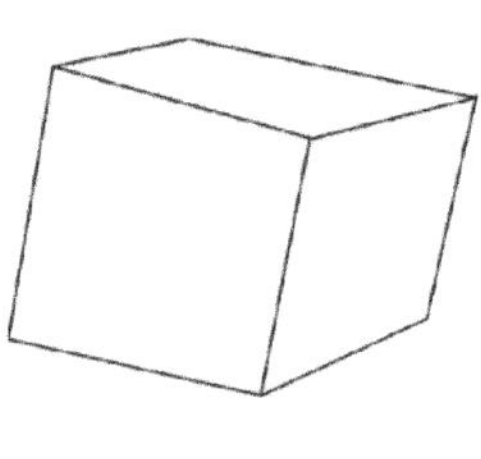 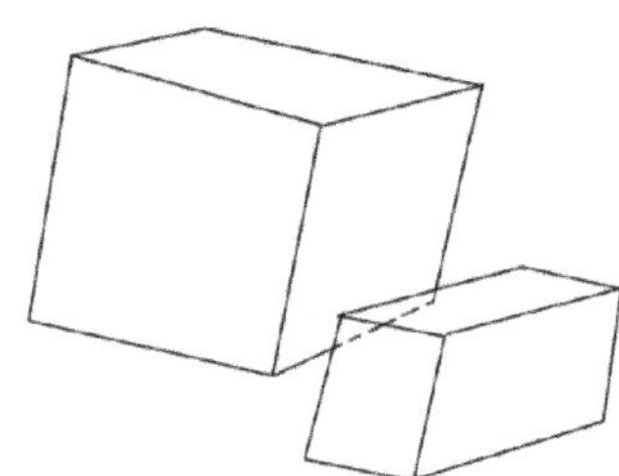 

1 FOLLOW THESE THREE SIMPLE STEPS TO FORM THE SHAPE OF HIS HEAD AND LEFT ARM.

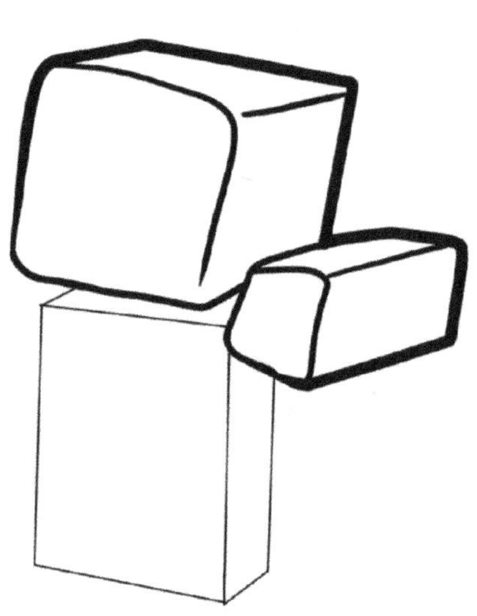 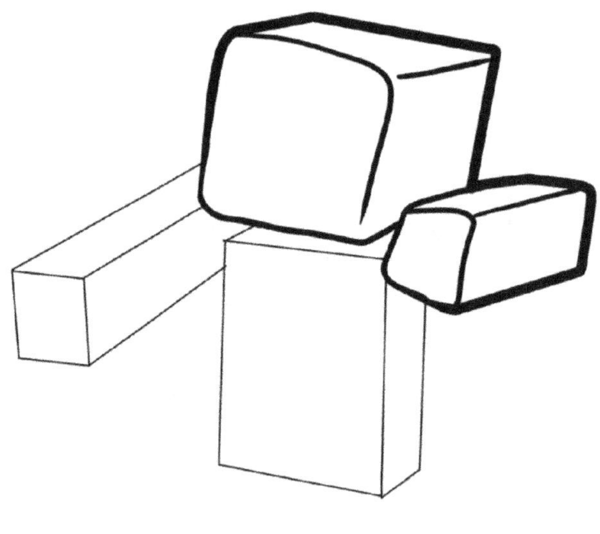

2 DRAW HIM A TORSO FOLLOWING THE IMAGE ABOVE.

3 NOW DRAW HIS RIGHT ARM.

ZOMBIE PIGMAN

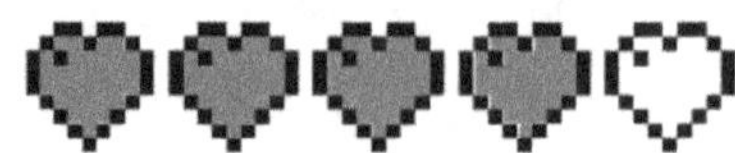

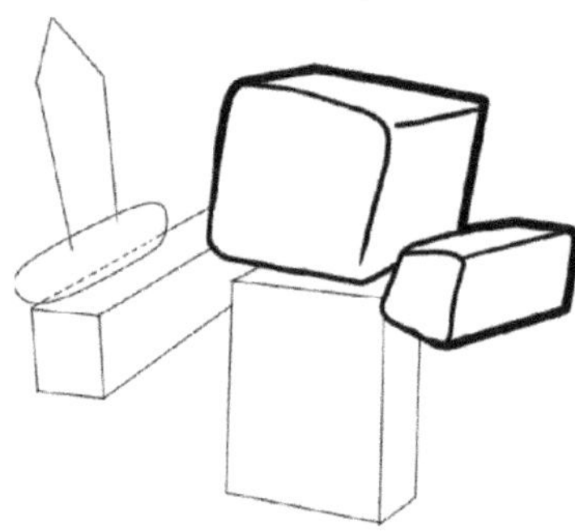

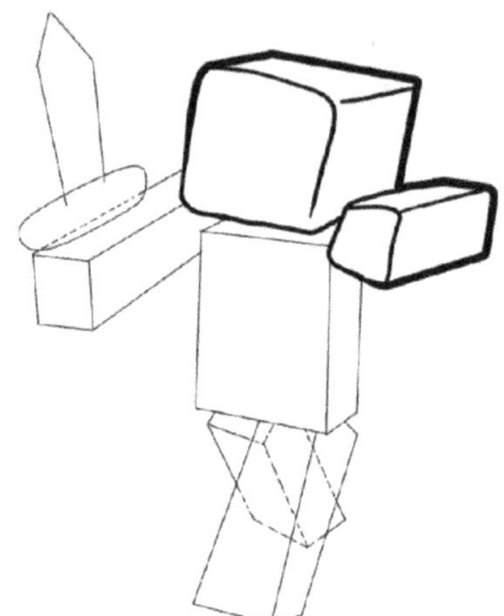

4 DRAW THE SHAPE OF A SWORD ON HIS RIGHT HAND.

5 LET'S PROCEED WITH HIS LEGS. FIRST, FORM THE LEFT LEG, THEN DRAW HIS RIGHT ONE BEHIND LEFT.

6 USE THICKER LINES TO DRAW HIS FINAL BODY SHAPE.

7 NOW, LET'S FINISH THIS DRAWING AND MAKE HIM LOOK CREEPY AND SCARY BY DRAWING HIS FACE AND ADDING DETAILS ON HIS BODY.

# SHEEP

## DIFFICULTY LEVEL

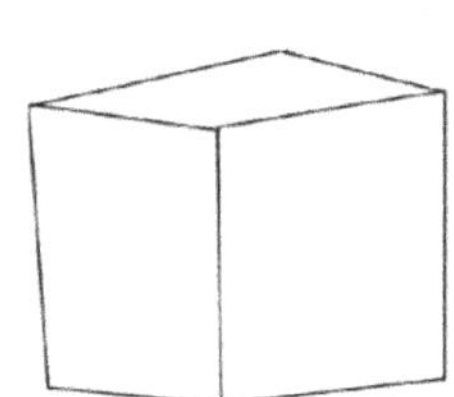
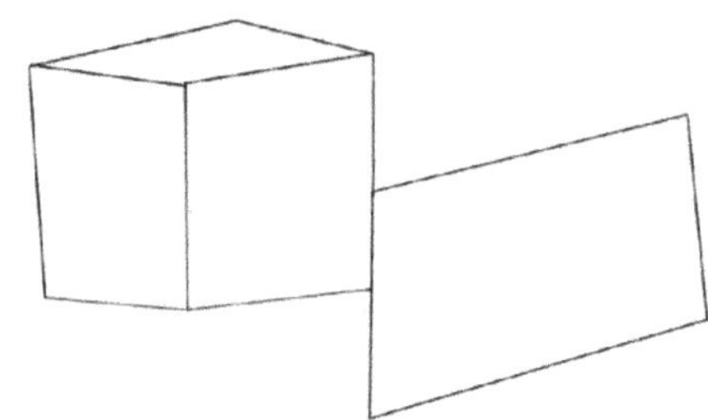

1 DRAW A CUBE. THEN DRAW A RECTANGLE BESIDE THE CUBE AS SHOWN IN OUR GUIDE.

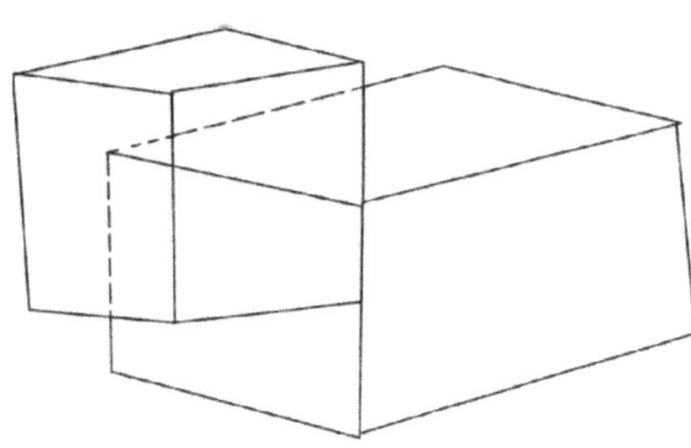

2 NOW ADD DIMENSIONS TO THE RECTANGLE TO CREATE A CUBOID. ERASE DOTTED LINES.

3 TO FORM SHEEP'S TORSO, FOLLOW THE GUIDE BELOW. DON'T WORRY, IT IS NOT THAT HARD. JUST RELAX AND FOLLOW THE DRAWING.

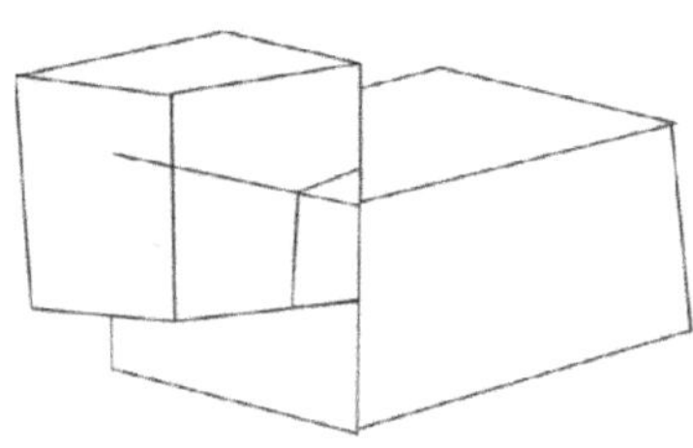
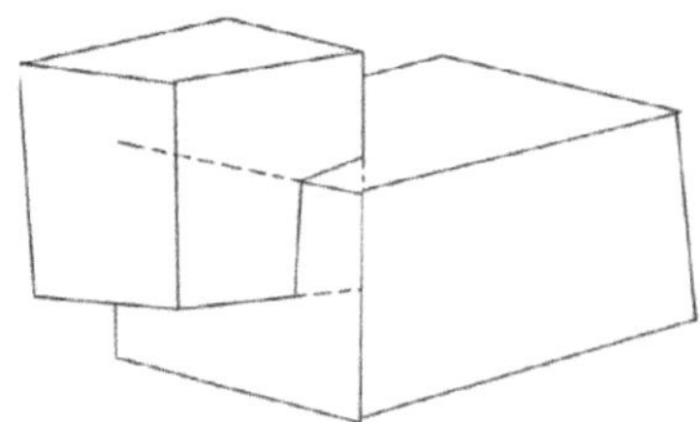
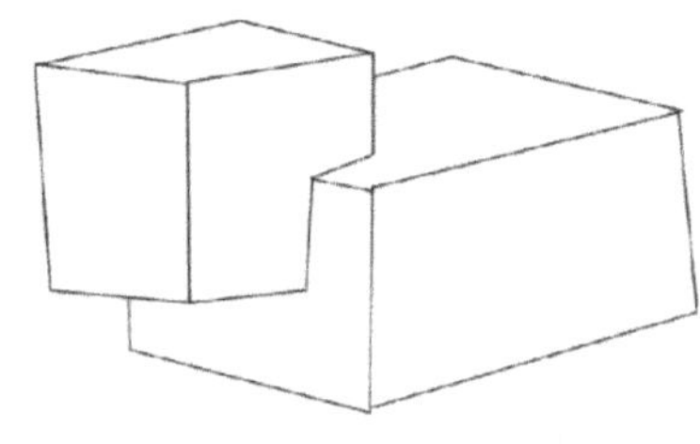

 SHEEP

DIFFICULTY LEVEL

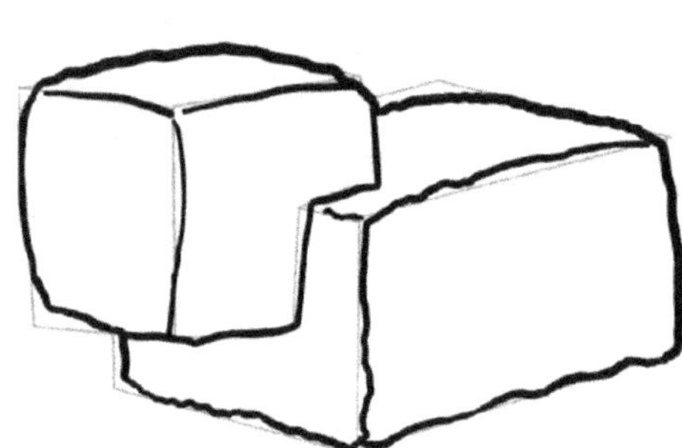

4 USE THICKER AND WIGGLY LINES TO DRAW THE FINAL SHAPE OF THE TORSO.

5 NOW WE CAN START FORMING THE SHEEP'S LEG. FOLLOW THE DRAWINGS BELOW. USE THICKER LINES TO TRACE THE FINAL SHAPE OF THE SHEEP'S LEGS.

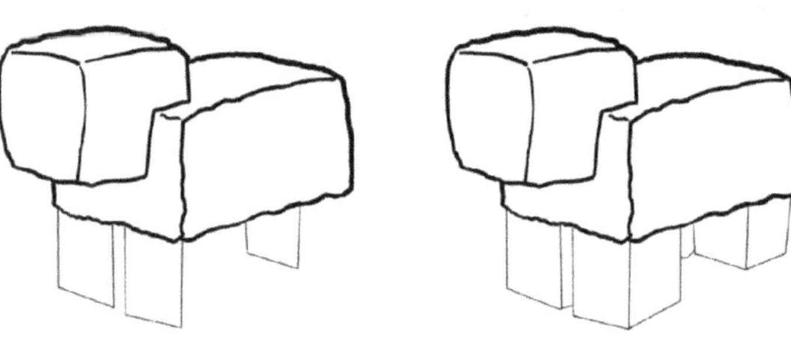

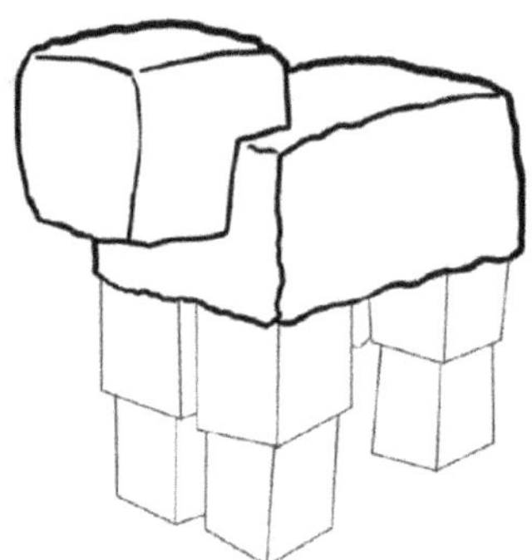

6 DRAW A FACE TO OUR SHEEP AND FEW DETAILS ON HER LEGS. MAKE HER FUR SOFT AND CURLY WITH THIN LINES.

POTION

1 TO DRAW A POTION, START WITH A SHAPE OF A BOTTLE. TRY TO DRAW SOMETHING LIKE THIS:

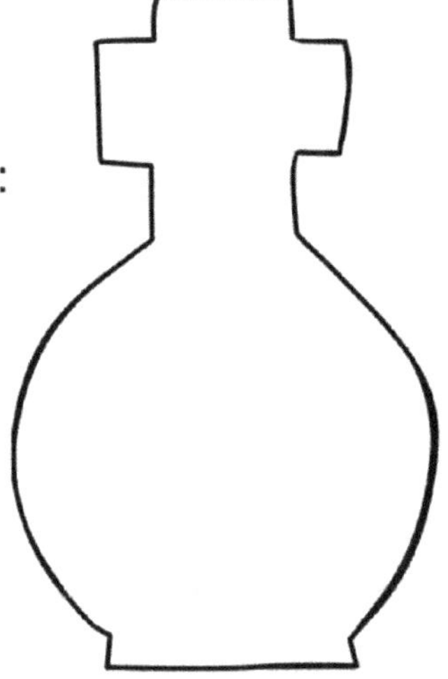

2 SEPARATE THE BOTTLE FROM THE CORK. DRAW A SHADING OF A GLASS REFLECTION ON THE BOTTLE.

3 YOU ARE ALMOST FINISHED! USE THINNER LINES TO DRAW SMALL DETAILS ON YOUR BOTTLE. COLOR IT AND THERE IT IS!